Philippians

A Digest of Reformed Comment

Philippians

A Digest of Reformed Comment

GEOFFREY B. WILSON
MINISTER OF BIRKBY BAPTIST CHURCH
HUDDERSFIELD

THE BANNER OF TRUTH TRUST

THE BANNER OF TRUTH TRUST
3 Murrayfield Road, Edinburgh EH12 6EL
P.O. Box 621, Carlisle, Pennsylvania 17013, USA

★

© 1983 Geoffrey Backhouse Wilson
First published 1983
ISBN 0 85151 363 8

★

Set in VIP Bembo
Filmset, printed and bound in Great Britain by
Hazell Watson & Viney Ltd
Aylesbury, Bucks

CONTENTS

PREFACE

In this short commentary I have tried to do justice to Paul's pastoral purpose in writing to the Philippians without altogether ignoring the many difficulties of the Epistle. I am grateful to the publishers who have given permission to quote from their works, and for the assistance received from Dr. Williams's Library. As usual the commentary is based on the American Standard Version (1901), published by Thomas Nelson Inc.

Huddersfield GEOFFREY WILSON
June 1982

INTRODUCTION

The city of Philippi derived its name from Philip II of Macedon, who refounded it in 356 BC and developed its gold-mining industry. In 167 BC it became part of the Roman Empire, and in 42 BC was the scene of the decisive battle in which Anthony and Octavian defeated Brutus and Cassius. After the war many veterans from the Roman army were settled there and the city was designated a Roman colony. As the citizens of such colonies were very proud of the special privileges conferred by their superior status, they 'were apt to regard themselves as being *in* but not *of* the province where they lay' (A. N. Sherwin-White).

However, when Paul and Silas came to Philippi in AD 50, their visit brought the city the greater distinction of being the first in Europe to hear the gospel from Paul's lips. In the first of the 'we' passages of *Acts* (16.10ff) Luke gives a vivid eye-witness account of the conversion of three founder-members of the Philippian church: Lydia the seller of purple, the demon-possessed slave-girl whom Paul had cured, and the jailor of the prison. But the church which first met as a small group in Lydia's house was soon to become a flourishing congregation with whom Paul had the happiest relations over many years. On more than one occasion they had shown their love for Paul by sending a gift to supply his material necessities (4.15, 16).

On learning of the apostle's imprisonment, the Christians at Philippi sent Epaphroditus to minister to his needs and bring a further gift (4.18). But this willing service was interrupted by a near fatal illness and, when Epaphroditus mercifully recovered, Paul deemed it best to send him back to Philippi with this joyous Epistle of thanksgiving (2.25–30). While writing Paul also took the opportunity to deal with several problems which threatened to mar the fellowship of the church. He tactfully seeks to heal a breach caused through a 'personality' clash (4.2), cuts the ground from under the feet of a 'perfectionist' pressure group (3.12–16), and warns against the danger of listening to the Judaizers (3.2f). Another purpose served by the letter was to give news of his current circumstances and of his hope of an early release from prison (1.25; 2.24). Where Paul was held captive when he wrote Philippians is a matter of debate, with some scholars favouring Ephesus or even Caesarea, but this commentary follows the traditional view of dating it from near the end of his first Roman imprisonment, about AD 62.

Notwithstanding J. A. Bengel's justly celebrated comment, 'The sum of the epistle is, *I rejoice, rejoice ye*', joy is not the theme of Philippians but is rather its dominant note. The whole letter is suffused with the spirit of joy, and the noun or verb occurs sixteen times in its four chapters. It is remarkable that a prisoner facing a capital charge should write in such a spirit, yet it is the very nature of Christian joy to triumph over adverse circumstances (cf *Acts* 16.25). So the Philippians are not exhorted to rejoice because of the happiness of their situation, but because whatever persecution they suffered for the sake of Christ was far outweighed by the joy they had found in him (1.27–30; 4.4–9).

By giving the Epistle the heading, 'The apostle and his

friends', the New English Bible draws attention to its leading theme, which is clearly seen in Paul's sustained emphasis upon 'fellowship' or 'communion'. The word basically means 'sharing in something with others', and it may be used to indicate either what is shared ('having a share') or what is given ('giving a share'). The first sense includes sharing in Christ's benefits (1.7), his indwelling power (2.1), and his sufferings (3.10), while the second sense involves making sacrifices to forward his work in the world (1.5). Thus the bond that binds Paul and the Philippians together in Christian fellowship is their common participation in Christ and the work of the 'gospel' (which is another keyword in the Epistle: 1.5, 7, 12, 27; 2.22; 4.3, 15). All this means that there can be no fellowship apart from joint communion with Christ, for it is in him alone that believers are truly made one.

But the outstanding feature of this lovely letter is the majestic 'hymn to Christ' in 2.6–11, which Paul introduces to provide the Christians at Philippi with both the pattern and the dynamic to comply with his exhortations. It is evident that the apostle's purpose is not simply to instruct and edify his readers with profound doctrine; his chief concern is to inspire and motivate them to show the same humility of mind (2.2). This is because Christians cannot work for Christ without also having the mind of Christ. And that involves showing the same spirit of self-denial which made him obedient 'unto death, even the death of the cross' (2.8).

CHAPTER ONE

After greeting the Christians at Philippi, Paul thanks God for their uninterrupted fellowship in the gospel, and confidently expects God to continue his good work in them until its completion in the day of Christ [vv 1–7]. He prays for an increase in their love and knowledge so that they may be made fit for the glory to come [vv 9–11]. The apostle tells how his imprisonment has helped to further the gospel by stimulating others to preach Christ, and though not all do so from the right motives, he still rejoices in the fact that Christ is preached [vv 12–18]. In facing an uncertain future, he is torn between the desire to depart and be with Christ and the need to remain, but he expects to be released for the sake of his assistance to them [vv 19–26]. Paul exhorts them to live worthily of the gospel, and to stand united in its defence, since it is not only given to them to believe on Christ but also to suffer for him [vv 27–30].

V 1: **Paul and Timothy, servants of Christ Jesus, to all the saints in Christ Jesus that are at Philippi, with the bishops and deacons:**

Paul associates Timothy with himself in the greeting, not because Timothy played any part in the composition of the letter as Paul's prompt return to the singular demonstrates [*v* 3], but because he wishes to prepare the Philippians for

Timothy's forthcoming visit [2.19ff] by showing them that they are colleagues engaged in the same work. This is further emphasized by the joint designation, 'bond servants of Christ Jesus' (F. F. Bruce), which is not an honorific title, but an expression denoting their complete submission to the lordship of Christ. Having been redeemed by Christ from the bondage of sin, they are now totally at the disposal of their new Master. The humility of this address would have special point for readers whose service was in danger of being marred by 'vainglory' [2.3]. 'Many who today love to be called "church workers" should learn what Paul means by "slaves", namely, men who in all their work have no will of their own but only their Owner's will and Word' (R. C. H. Lenski).

to all the saints in Christ Jesus that are at Philippi,
Under the Old Covenant Israel was 'holy' in the sense of having been 'set apart' for God's service [*Deut* 7.6], whereas the gift of holiness is actually conferred upon the beneficiaries of the New Covenant. *All* believers not only have the standing of 'saints' in virtue of their spiritual union with Christ, but are also objectively 'holy' in him because his perfect righteousness is freely put to their account [3.9; 1 *Cor* 1.30; 2 *Cor* 5.21]. 'We do not progress *to* sainthood. We progress *in* sainthood. We progress in sainthood in proportion as we sing alleluias for the initial gift of sainthood' (F. C. Synge). This heavenly union with Christ is here contrasted with the earthly location of the worshipping community. The saints at Philippi are the free-born citizens of heaven [3.20], but their present vocation is to bear witness to Christ amid the pagan darkness of a Roman colony [1 *Pet* 2.9].

with the bishops and deacons: Presumably Paul singles out these men for special mention because they took the lead in sending assistance to him [4.10–16]. The terms 'elder' and 'bishop' are used interchangeably in the New Testament, the former indicating status, the latter function [cf *Tit* 1.5–7]. The work entrusted to the 'bishops' (or 'overseers') was the pastoral care of the flock [*Acts* 20.28], while the duties of 'deacons' were chiefly concerned with the administration and finances of the church.

*V*2: **Grace to you and peace from God our Father and the Lord Jesus Christ.**

In combining the usual Greek and Hebrew forms of greeting, Paul gives them a distinctively Christian content, in which 'grace' points to the undeserved favour of God made known in the Lord Jesus Christ, and 'peace' includes the salvation of the whole man which results from the reception of this grace. These blessings are jointly bestowed by the God whom believers know as their Father, and by their Saviour who is now the ascended Lord of the church [2.9–11].

*V*3: **I thank my God upon all my remembrance of you, 4 always in every supplication of mine on behalf of you all making my supplication with joy, 5 for your fellowship in furtherance of the gospel from the first day until now; 6 being confident of this very thing, that he who began a good work in you will perfect it until the day of Jesus Christ:**

There are more frequent references to thanksgiving per page in Paul's letters than can be found in any other

[17]

Hellenistic author, pagan or Christian[1]. This is because Paul knew that such gratitude was the only appropriate response which could be made to the gift of God's grace. In most of his Epistles Paul begins with a thanksgiving that reflects the situation of his readers and serves to introduce the main theme of the letter. Here, for example, the apostle strikes the keynote of the first two chapters by thanking God for the fellowship of the faithful Philippians in furthering the work of the gospel [v 5]. He thus has special cause for gratitude as he regularly remembers them in his prayers and makes supplication for them *all* with joy. Paul's studied repetition of the word 'all' in his opening sentences is remarkable [1.1, 4, 7, 8, 25], and J. B. Lightfoot says that it is 'impossible not to connect this recurrence of the word with the strong and repeated exhortations to unity which the epistle contains [1.27; 2.1–4; 4.2, 3, 5, 7, 9]'. But though Paul was not blind to the failings that needed correction, he could never pray for his friends at Philippi without being filled with joy at the remembrance of their continued participation in the gospel, which was tangibly expressed in their generous giving [cf 2 *Cor* 8.1–5]. Moreover, they began to share in this work from the first day they received the gospel. 'The communion of the saints was with them a point of practice as well as an article of belief' (John Trapp). Such consistent conduct made Paul confident that the Philippians were the subjects of a genuine work of grace. As their good works were the evidence of God's 'good work' in them, so Paul assures them that God who began that gracious work 'will carry it on to completion until the day of Christ Jesus' (NIV). As well as conveying comfort to believers facing persecution

1. P. T. O'Brien, 'Thanksgiving within the Structure of Pauline Theology', *Pauline Studies*, pp. 54–63.

[1.27–30], this assurance also demolishes the pretensions of those who imagined that they had already attained perfection [cf 3.12–16]. 'It is on the second advent of Christ – and that is the end of the world, and the judgment day – that the Apostle has his eyes set. There is the point of time to which he refers the completeness of our perfecting' (B. B. Warfield). [cf 1 *Thess* 5.23–24].

*V*7: **even as it is right for me to be thus minded on behalf of you all, because I have you in my heart, inasmuch as, both in my bonds and in the defence and confirmation of the gospel, ye are all partakers with me of grace.**

It is only right for Paul to think so highly of the Philippians, because he regards them in his heart as all being partakers with him of God's grace, both in his bonds and in his defence and confirmation of the gospel. This praise was well deserved. 'For it is much not to hide oneself when a Christian is called to account for the sake of the gospel; it is much when those who are in the same place where he is detained have the courage to remain there, without withdrawing themselves from the danger by flight; it is still more when they dare see and strengthen him, paying him the attentions of love on such an occasion. But it is much more than all this, to seek after him at a distance, to traverse the sea to console him, and not only not to fly away from the place of his prison, but to run thither, and to go many hundreds of leagues to declare themselves on his side. This the Philippians had done, when, having been made acquainted with the detention of St. Paul at Rome, they despatched Epaphroditus to visit and to minister to him on their behalf' (Jean Daillé). Hence the help they sent to the imprisoned apostle together with their willingness to suffer persecution at home for the sake of the gospel showed that they were truly partakers with Paul of God's grace [1.29]. It is probably best to take 'the defence and confirmation of the gospel' in the technical legal sense. Paul sees his witness at his forthcoming trial as a legal validation of the gospel which will receive further confirmation in his acquittal [2.24].

*V*8: **For God is my witness, how I long after you all in the tender mercies of Christ Jesus.**

As no words can adequately express Paul's yearning for his beloved friends at Philippi, he solemnly appeals to the fact that God who reads every heart, knows the depth and intensity of his feeling for them all. This longing is not mere human affection, but is a love which is the fruit of his spiritual union with Christ, so that 'his pulse beats with the pulse of Christ; his heart throbs with the heart of Christ' (Lightfoot). As a man who is 'in Christ', Paul is gripped by the same love which Christ has for his people, and every true pastor feels something of this affection for the flock committed to his care.

*V*9: **And this I pray, that your love may abound yet more and more in knowledge and all discernment; 10 so that ye may approve the things that are excellent; that ye may be sincere and void of offence unto the day of Christ; 11 being filled with the fruits of righteousness, which are through Jesus Christ, unto the glory and praise of God.**

Paul's prayers for the churches not only provide the pattern on which their own petitions are to be modelled, but also encourage them to follow the counsel they contain. They are thus a form of indirect exhortation. Hence this particular prayer focuses on those aspects of faith and life which most needed to be stressed at Philippi.

And this I pray, that your love may abound yet more and more in knowledge and all discernment; Paul first prays for an increase in the primary Christian grace of love [1 *Cor* 13.13], already experienced in love towards God and in their mutual love for one another, so that they may abound more and more. But this request is immediately qualified by the phrase, 'in knowledge and all discernment', for even Christian love may go badly astray unless it is directed aright. 'Misty thought, emotional conduct, and indiscriminate good nature are perilous' (Alfred Plummer). It would seem that the enthusiastic spirit which prevailed in this church was accompanied by a lack of insight. This led to misunderstandings over trifling matters [cf 4.2], and to giving heed to plausible teachers [cf 3.1–3, 17–19].

so that ye may approve the things that are excellent; 'Not merely good, rather than bad, but the best among the good, whose excellence none but the more advanced perceive' (J. A. Bengel). Some prefer the rendering, 'so that ye may distinguish the things that differ' (ASV margin), but it does not require much discernment to discriminate between what is good and bad. It is far more difficult to decide what is really excellent and worthy of adoption [cf 4.8, 9]. Paul is praying that his readers may be enabled to discern and practise those virtues which are vital to the peace and harmony of the church [2.1–3].

that ye may be sincere and void of offence unto the day of Christ; Thus to relate ethics to the End adds an eternal dimension to present conduct. The Philippians must so live in the light of the forthcoming judgment that they will be 'sincere and void of offence' on 'the day of Christ' [2 *Cor* 5.10]. The word translated as 'sincere' probably means 'tested by the light of the sun' and found 'completely pure' or 'spotless'. This inward purity results in a harmless walk, for 'void of offence' should be understood in the active sense of not causing others to stumble [1 *Cor* 10.32]. 'The possession of love, and the growth of it in knowledge and discernment, would prevent them from rudely jostling others not of their opinion, or doing anything which, (albeit) with a good intention, might mislead or throw a stumbling-block in the path of those round about them' (John Eadie).

being filled with the fruits of righteousness, which are through Jesus Christ, This further desire of the apostle for his readers again applies to their present experience. As befits 'the saints' [*v* 1], he wishes to see them 'being filled with the fruit of righteousness' (asv margin). There are two ways of interpreting this difficult phrase. If taken as 'the fruit which consists of righteousness', it means that their lives will be marked by those ethical qualities which are 'the fruit of the Spirit' [*Gal* 5.22f]. But when understood as 'the fruit produced by righteousness', it points to the imputed righteousness of Christ as the source of this fruit-bearing [3.9]. Perhaps the Old Testament origin of the phrase [cf *Amos* 6.12] should incline us to favour the former view instead of restricting 'righteousness' to its forensic meaning. In any case Paul makes it clear that 'the branch cannot bear fruit of itself' by showing that such fruits are

the natural and necessary consequence of union with Christ
('which are through Jesus Christ').

unto the glory and praise of God. Since this spiritual
harvest is not a human achievement but the gift of grace, all
the glory and praise belong to God [2.11]. As God's 'glory'
here refers to the manifestation of his character in redemption, so his 'praise' is the response which that revelation
evokes in grateful human hearts [cf *Eph* 1.6, 12].

V 12: **Now I would have you know, brethren, that the
things** *which happened* **unto me have fallen out rather
unto the progress of the gospel;**

As the Philippians were anxiously awaiting news of their
beloved apostle, Paul wants his brethren in the faith to
know that the things which have happened to him in Rome
have furthered rather then hindered the advance of the
gospel. He thus characteristically dwells not on his personal
circumstances, about which his readers both then and now
would have liked to know more, but concentrates their
attention upon the supreme importance of the cause to
which he had devoted his life [*v* 17]. Apparently at the
time Paul wrote this letter, he no longer enjoyed the
comparative freedom of his hired lodging [*Acts* 28.30] and
was held in stricter custody as he awaited the verdict of his
trial, which would either result in his release or his death
[*vv* 19–26; 2.17]. But Paul is far from feeling downcast by
this turn of events, for he can perceive that God has made
his very imprisonment a means of promoting the faith. It
is always God's way to make what threatens to suppress the
gospel minister to its advance. The long confinement in
Bedford gaol which silenced John Bunyan's preaching only

served to make him an evangelist to the whole world through his writing of *The Pilgrim's Progress*. Thus God constantly turns the seeming defeat of his spokesmen into notable victories for the gospel by his providential over-ruling of such opposition [*Gen* 45.8].

V 13: **so that my bonds became manifest in Christ throughout the whole praetorian guard, and to all the rest;**

Paul next explains how the gospel has been advanced. His imprisonment has influenced both those outside the church [*v* 13] and those within it [*v* 14]. It has become very clear to all that his bonds are not the result of any criminal activity; they are manifestly due to his connection with Christ. 'Waiting under an appeal to the emperor, he had been discovered to be no common prisoner. It had tran-spired that his official connection with Christ, and his fearless prosecution of the work of Christ, had led to his apprehension and previous trial in Palestine, and not sedition, turbulence, or suspected loyalty – the usual political crimes of his nation. It was widely known that he suffered as a Christian and as an apostle, especially as the preacher of a free and unconditioned gospel to the Gentiles' (Eadie).

throughout the whole praetorian guard, and to all the rest; The 'praetorium' cannot here refer to a palace or barracks, because 'all the rest' clearly indicates that Paul has a group of people in view, namely, the élite soldiers of the imperial guard who were stationed at Rome. The whole praetorian guard consisted of nine cohorts with a 1000 men in each. As the guards who watched over the prisoners were frequently changed, Paul came into close contact with a large number of these men during the years of his captivity, and such was the impression he made upon them that his case was soon 'headline' news in Rome.

V 14: **and that most of the brethren in the Lord, being confident through my bonds, are more abundantly bold to speak the word of God without fear.**

and most of the brethren have been made confident in the Lord because of my imprisonment, and are much more bold to speak the word of God without fear. (RSV) As the phrase 'in the Lord' lies between 'the brethren' and 'being confident' it can be connected with either, but the latter construction is preferable because it is more in accord with Pauline usage [cf 2.24; *Rom* 14.14; *Gal* 5.10; 2 *Thess* 3.4]. Paul's imprisonment also advanced the gospel by the favourable effect it had upon the majority of believers in Rome. Their confidence in the Lord was renewed through his courageous testimony, and they were thus emboldened to speak the word of God without fear. They had hitherto preached with some caution, but the brave example set by the apostle now inspired them to speak with far greater daring. Trapp illustrates this verse by quoting from a letter of Bishop Ridley to John Bradford in which he describes his reaction to the death of John Rogers, the first Protestant martyr in Mary's bloody reign: 'I thank our Lord God that since I heard of our dear brother Rogers' departing, and stout confessing of Christ and his truth even unto death, my heart, blessed be God, rejoiced of it; neither ever since that time I have felt any lumpish heaviness, as I grant I have felt sometimes before'.

[25]

*V*15: **Some indeed preach Christ even of envy and strife; and some also of good will:** 16 **the one** *do it* **of love, knowing that I am set for the defence of the gospel;** 17 **but the other proclaim Christ of faction, not sincerely, thinking to raise up affliction for me in my bonds.**

'We have here a second paradox. It was paradoxical that the imprisonment of the Apostle should tend to the spread of the Gospel. It was a still greater paradox that the Gospel of love and peace should be preached out of envy and strife' (Plummer). Paul sadly records that among the many thus stimulated to preach Christ with increased boldness, there were some whose zeal sprang from the wrong motives. Since he does not accuse them of false teaching, they are not the Judaizers whom he later so unsparingly condemns [3.2] and elsewhere describes as preaching a different gospel [*Gal* 1.6–9]. As to a more positive identification of these men, Eadie suggests that they were Jewish believers, who held the essential doctrines of the gospel, but were combative on points of inferior value [cf *Rom* 14]. If what united them was their opposition to the apostle of Gentile freedom, 'then such a party might preach Christ, and yet cherish toward Paul all those feelings of envy and ill-will which he ascribes to them'.

Some indeed preach Christ even of envy and strife; and some also of good will: 'The Lord taketh notice, not only of the matter which ministers do preach, whether it be truth or error; but also of the manner how, the ends for which, and the motives from which they preach: even whether they preach Christ "from envy and contention, or

from love and good will''; for here Paul taketh notice of it'
(James Fergusson).

**the one *do it* of love, knowing that I am set for the
defence of the gospel;** Those 'of good will' exercise a
ministry which stems from a love of real understanding,
which recognizes that the imprisoned apostle is set like a *e*
soldier at his post for the defence of the gospel, and is as
much 'on duty' as the guards who watch over him (R. P.
Martin). They knew that he was a willing sufferer for the
cause he represented. 'These brethren did not merely "like"
Paul; they saw what his office and his imprisonment meant
in the plans of God and acted accordingly' (Lenski).

**but the other proclaim Christ of faction, not sincerely,
thinking to raise up affliction for me in my bonds.**
But the others, who are envious of Paul's prestige and
influence, proclaim Christ in a spirit of rivalry born of
selfish ambition, and not from pure motives, thinking that
this will add to his distress in prison. 'They attributed their
own jealous feelings to the Apostle, and could not conceive
a greater worry to him than that he should hear of their
success in preaching' (H. A. A. Kennedy).

*V*18: **What then? only that in every way, whether in
pretence or in truth, Christ is proclaimed; and therein
I rejoice, yea, and will rejoice.**

But what does it matter? (NIV) Paul's magnanimity is
seen in his refusal to allow the personal antagonism towards
himself on the part of some preachers to cloud his joy in the
only thing that mattered – Christ is proclaimed! 'In pretence' does not mean that these men did not believe what

they were preaching, but rather refers to their insincerity in preaching Christ to discomfort Paul [*v* 17]. Although the apostle could never rejoice in the preaching of error, he is resolved to rejoice in the preaching of Christ even if it proceeds from impure motives, because he recognized that the power to save lies in the gospel and not the gospeller (Eadie). As Daillé observes, It is not enough that our actions be good and praiseworthy, if our intentions are not pure and upright. It is to profane the good to do it with a bad end in view, but 'while we detest the abominable profaneness of men who so dreadfully abuse the gospel, let us not cease to rejoice at the good effects which God produces by their hands. Let us hold the thorns of such plants in horror, and gather with thanksgiving the roses which the goodness of God causes to spring from them; and, after the example of the apostle, let us rejoice to see our Christ preached, whatever may be the mind or the hand which presents us His mysteries'.

*V*19: **For I know that this shall turn out to my salvation, through your supplication and the supply of the Spirit of Jesus Christ,**

Paul is confident that the present situation in which he finds himself shall turn out for his salvation. This citation from Job shows that the apostle sees a parallel to his own experience in the testimony of that much tried Old Testament saint. The whole context deserves to be quoted:

'Hold your peace, let me alone, that I may speak;
And let come on me what will.
Wherefore should I take my flesh in my teeth,
And put my life in my hand?

[28]

Though he slay me, yet will I wait for him.
Nevertheless I will argue my ways before him.
This also *shall be my salvation*,
That a godless man shall not come before him.'

[*Job* 13.13–16: ASV margin]

Although Job and Paul are both on trial, neither has in mind a salvation which guarantees his deliverance from death, for Job says: 'though he slay me', and Paul: 'whether by life, or by death' [*v* 20]. They are saved from something far worse than this. Job appeals to God for vindication from the accusations of his false comforters, and Paul desires to be saved from disgracing Christ before the Imperial court. 'Paul says that he knows he will be saved from anything like this. By *this* he refers to his trial: this will turn out safely for him so that he will not disgrace the gospel through cowardice, fear, lack of free utterance, or any inadequacy' (Lenski).

through your supplication and the supply of the Spirit of Jesus Christ, Paul does not say this in any spirit of self-sufficiency, for he expects his deliverance to come through the prayers of the Philippians and the supply of 'the Spirit of Jesus Christ'. The Spirit is sent by Christ so that Paul can witness to Christ in the hour of trial [*Mark* 13.11; *Luke* 12.11, 12].

V 20: **according to my earnest expectation and hope, that in nothing shall I be put to shame, but *that* with all boldness, as always, *so* now also Christ shall be magnified in my body, whether by life, or by death.**

The eagerness with which Paul looks for the vindication of

the gospel at his trial is vividly expressed by 'earnest expectation'. The word is well defined by Kennedy as 'the concentrated intense hope which ignores other interests, and strains forward as with outstretched head' [cf *Rom* 8.19]. The content of this hope is next specified. It is that he may face his ordeal with such courage that he will have no cause to be ashamed, but may be enabled to bear witness to Christ with all the boldness and openness of speech which should characterize one who enjoys the liberty of the Spirit [2 *Cor* 3.12]. Whatever the result of the trial may mean for Paul, his desire now as always is that 'Christ shall be magnified in my body'. He does not say what *he* will do, but uses the passive because he is relying upon the supply of the Spirit for the achievement of this great end [*v* 19]. So whether the verdict is life or death, the glory of Christ will be promoted and his gospel advanced. 'If he lives, it will be for the service of Christ, which is the highest honour he can pay his Lord. If he has to die, then his readiness to endure death, and his calm courage in enduring, will be the most eloquent testimony to the worth of his Lord' (Kennedy).

*V*21: **For me to live is Christ, and to die is gain.**

Paul's equanimity in facing these alternatives is explained in a great utterance: 'For *to me* to live is Christ, and to die is gain'. In his experience the only 'life' worthy of the name was that lived in union with Christ and spent in his service, and so for him 'death' was gain because it gave entrance to the immediate presence of Christ. Thus to depart and be 'with Christ' in glory is better by far for Paul [*v* 23], but he recognizes that for him to continue living in the flesh may be more needful for his readers [*v* 24]. This passage, together with Christ's assurance to the penitent thief, 'Today shalt thou be with me in paradise' [*Luke* 23.43], are both fatal to the view that the intermediate state is one of sleep and unconsciousness. Paul knew that to be at home in the body was to be absent from the Lord, and so he was willing to be absent from the body in order to be 'at home with the Lord' [2 *Cor* 5.6–8]. 'The souls of believers are at their death made perfect in holiness, and do immediately pass into glory; and their bodies, being still united to Christ, do rest in their graves till the resurrection' (*The Shorter Catechism*, Answer to Question 37). [Cf *Heb* 12.23: 'the spirits of just men made perfect'.]

*V*22: **But if to live in the flesh, —*if* this shall bring fruit from my work, then what I shall choose I know not.**

If it is to be life in the flesh, that means fruitful labour for me. (RSV) But though death holds no terror for Paul, he does not want the Philippians to suppose that he is simply yearning for death, since a continuance of his earthly life is probably best both for him and them. The significance of Paul's statement lies in the fact that he regards a further lease of life exclusively in terms of bringing forth more fruit. For him 'life in the flesh' was synonymous with 'fruitful labour'. As all his previous missionary service had been blessed with an abundance of fruit, so his one reason for desiring an acquittal was that he might then continue his fruitful labours.

Yet which I shall choose I cannot tell. (RSV) If Paul had to choose between promotion to glory and a period of further service, he would not know what to decide. Thus Trapp quaintly says, 'As a loving wife sent for by her husband far from home, and yet loath to leave her children, is in a muse and doubt what to do, so was the apostle'.

*V*23: **But I am in a strait betwixt the two, having the desire to depart and be with Christ; for it is very far better: 24 yet to abide in the flesh is more needful for your sake.**

In describing his dilemma, Paul says that he is 'hemmed in on both sides' (Lightfoot). He has the desire 'to depart' (literally, to break camp) and be with Christ, for that is 'very far better' (a triple comparative!). 'The preference of death over life was a personal matter. It was better for him; far better for him to be with Christ, than to be away from Christ; far better to enjoy Christ than to preach Christ; far better to praise Him than to suffer for Him; far better to be in His presence in glory, than to be bound in a prison for Him at Rome' (Eadie). But Paul always put his 'concern for all the churches' [2 *Cor* 11.28, NIV] before personal considerations, and he knew that it was more necessary for them that he should remain in the body. The contrast between these alternatives is helpfully set forth by William Hendriksen:

Remaining here and	*Departing to be with Christ*
Here:	There:
a. A temporary residence, a mere tent-dwelling	A permanent abode
b. Suffering mixed with joy	Joy unmixed with suffering
c. Suffering for a little while	Joy for ever
d. Being absent from the Lord	Being at home with the Lord
e. The fight	The feast
f. The realm of sin	The realm of complete deliverance from sin, positive holiness

*V*25: **And having this confidence, I know that I shall abide, yea, and abide with you all, for your progress and joy in the faith;**

Although this personal conviction does not amount to prophetic certainty, Paul 'is so confident of the Philippians' need of him that he cannot doubt that this will be God's purpose too' (Kennedy). He will remain alive and stay to serve them, for the sake of their further progress in the faith. His personal longing to depart and be with Christ is thus subordinated to the church's need of his continued ministry. This service would be aimed at forwarding their 'progress and joy in the faith'. The linking together of 'progress' and 'joy' is significant, for it shows that every advance in the faith should be accompanied by a corresponding increase in joy. We know from the Pastoral Epistles that Paul's confidence was justified. He was released and entered upon another term of service before his final imprisonment and martyrdom [2 *Tim* 4.6–8].

*V*26: **that your glorying may abound in Christ Jesus in me through my presence with you again.**

so that in me you may have ample cause to glory in Christ Jesus, because of my coming to you again. (RSV) When Paul is restored to the Philippians and his ministry among them is renewed, their ground for glorying will be increased by what Christ has done for them through his servant. For the ultimate aim of all ministry is to give further cause for glorying in Christ Jesus. Thus to glory in Christ Jesus means the abandonment of all self-boasting, for unlike the merit-mongers who trust in the flesh, believers are so radically committed to Christ that even the last vestige of trust in themselves is excluded [cf 3.3: 'we . . . glory in Christ Jesus, and have no confidence in the flesh']. But the prospect of ministering to them again in the future does not deter Paul from his present duty. So he turns from this happy prospect and sends them the exhortations and instructions which are necessary to deal with the pressing problems they are now facing [1.27ff].

V27: **Only let your manner of life be worthy of the gospel of Christ: that, whether I come and see you or be absent, I may hear of your state, that ye stand fast in one spirit, with one soul striving for the faith of the gospel;**

Standing emphatically at the beginning of the sentence, 'Only' points to the one essential thing which demands the Philippians' immediate attention, no matter what happens to Paul. The verb which is translated as 'let your manner of life be' literally means 'behave as citizens' (ASV margin). The fact that Paul later alludes to their heavenly citizenship [3.20] strongly suggests that he has the same idea in mind here. He wants their life as a Christian community to be worthy of the gospel of Christ. 'The exhortation contemplates the Philippians as members of the Christian *commonwealth*. The figure would be naturally suggested to Paul by his residence in Rome, and would appeal to the Philippians as a Roman colony, which was a reproduction of the parent commonwealth on a smaller scale' (Marvin R. Vincent, *Word Studies in the New Testament*, Vol. II, p. 876). In view of the tensions within the church which threatened to mar their witness, Paul's one concern, whether present or absent, is to hear of their united stand for the truth of the gospel against 'the adversaries' [*v* 28] who oppose it [cf

Jude 3: 'contend earnestly for the faith which was once for all delivered unto the saints']. Since the call to stand fast 'in one spirit' is further defined as a striving together 'with one soul', no sharp distinction can be drawn between these terms, which are here virtually used as synonyms in order to underline the need for spiritual unity [cf *Acts* 4.32]. They must stand fast, like soldiers 'fighting side by side' (Moffatt). This vivid image would remind the Philippians of the phalanx, which consisted of a body of highly trained spearmen who fought together in closed ranks, for this was the tactic which was used by Philip of Macedon and his son Alexander the Great to achieve their great victories. 'The same spirit of unity and valour which had infused the phalanx sent forth for world conquest must now be evidenced by the members of the Church as they contend for the faith of the gospel' (W. L. Lane).

*V*28: **and in nothing affrighted by the adversaries: which is for them an evident token of perdition, but of your salvation, and that from God;**

and in no way intimidated by your opponents: (Arndt-Gingrich) This is the only occurrence in Scripture of a verb which was used for the shying of a frightened horse. The Philippians must not be thrown into a panic by their persecutors, but must face them without fear. As it would appear from *Acts* 16.13 that there were not enough Jews in Philippi to form a synagogue (a minimum of ten men was required), this opposition must have come mainly from their pagan neighbours, whose devotion to the heathen cults would have been affronted by a faith which condemned all idol-worship. Paul says that such Christian fearlessness under attack provides these persecutors with a token which

[35]

not only foreshadows their own doom but also points to the salvation of their victims. For in fighting against God's people they are bringing upon themselves that just recompense which consists in 'everlasting destruction from the presence of the Lord' [cf 2 *Thess* 1.5–9].

and that from God; This shows that God is the author of the Philippians' stability under suffering: 'their standing firm in contending and being unafraid comes to them "from God" even as Paul adds "graciously granted to you" [*v* 29]' (Lenski).

*V*29: **because to you it hath been granted in the behalf of Christ, not only to believe on him, but also to suffer in his behalf:**

Although Paul's primary concern here is to assure his readers that it is no less a privilege to suffer for Christ than to believe in him [*Acts* 5.41], his words also indicate that the prior grace of faith is just as much a gift of God [*Eph* 2.8]. 'He says expressly, "*that it is given us to believe in Christ*", which necessarily implies that this movement itself of our heart, opening to the light of the gospel, and receiving the truth that the preacher presents to it, is a gift of God, and not a work of nature . . . It is He who opened the heart of Lydia to attend to St. Paul [*Acts* 16.14]. Paul plants, and Apollos waters; but they are neither of them any thing. It is God which giveth the increase. We are His husbandry, and His work [1 *Cor* 3.6, 7, 9]. It is He who revealed His secret to Peter; it was not flesh and blood [*Matt* 16.17]. It is He who revealed His Son to Paul, shining in his heart, that he might enlighten the Gentiles [*Gal* 1.15]. In fine, it is He who, according to His good pleasure, hides these things from the wise and prudent, and reveals them unto babes [*Matt* 11.25]' (Daillé).

As to the privilege of suffering, Paul everywhere teaches that this is an essential part of the believer's experience and the badge of authentic discipleship [cf 3.10; *Acts* 14.22; *Rom* 5.3; 8.17, 35; 2 *Tim* 1.8]. This means that 'the persecution of believers is not a fortuitous event, which happens either by chance, or by the malice of men or devils alone. It is God, who guides the whole affair by a special providence. He sees the rage of the enemies of His people. He knows their designs, He perceives all that they are contriving against the gospel, and could (if such were His good pleasure) dissipate both their plans and their efforts in an instant. He lets them alone, and by secret arrangements manages their violence against every one of His servants, as His supreme wisdom sees best. He Himself marks the field where the combat is to be decided. He orders the weapons and the blows, and rules every action. He calls His warrior, and Himself places him in front of the enemy.

'Christian, do not stop at men, and at the appearance of things. Be convinced that it is the Lord who arranges all your trials. You will enter into none but by His permission. But the apostle also shows us, in the second place, that this employment which God gives us, and this calling which He directs us to suffer for Him, is a gift of His grace. I well know that flesh forms quite another judgment, and that of all the favours of God, there is none that it esteems and desires less than this . . . But, if, setting aside the tenderness of the flesh, you will consider the thing itself, what can be esteemed more honourable than suffering for the name of the Lord Jesus? This Jesus is the King of ages, the Prince of angels, the Lord of glory. His gospel is the highest of all truth, it is the salvation of the world, the seed of life and

immortality. For what better subject then could we suffer?'
(Daillé).

*V*30: **having the same conflict which ye saw in me,
and now hear to be in me.**

The Philippians are engaged in the same conflict which
they had seen in Paul when he suffered stripes and imprisonment at Philippi [*Acts* 16.19–24], and now hear about his
present imprisonment and trial in Rome [*v* 12; 2.25]. They
stand together in the great contest of faith to defend the
gospel of Christ against their common enemy. For they
wrestle not against flesh and blood, but against the powers
of darkness whose doom is already sealed by Christ's great
victory [*Eph* 6.12; *Col* 2.15]. Paul here 'thinks of the
conflicts and sufferings of the Christian life itself as a life
which in its totality stands under the sign of the cross and
in this sign carries the cause of Christ to victory' (E.
Stauffer, *TDNT*, Vol. I, p. 139).

CHAPTER TWO

Paul earnestly admonishes the Philippians to maintain the unity of the church by sharing the same mind, which above all consists in humility and selfless concern for their fellow-believers [vv 1–4]. This exhortation is enforced by an appeal to the example of Christ in a lofty passage which celebrates his self-denying love in taking the form of a servant and becoming obedient to the death of the cross, from which God had raised him to the seat of universal sovereignty [vv 5–11]. So they are to work out their own salvation in humble dependence upon God. This involves refraining from disputes and living so blamelessly that Paul would have no cause to be ashamed of them in the day of Christ [vv 12–18]. Paul hopes to send Timothy to Philippi shortly and warmly praises his fidelity. Meanwhile Epaphroditus, now happily recovered from his illness, is returning with this Epistle, and is to be duly honoured for risking his life in Paul's service [vv 19–30].

V 1: **If there is therefore any exhortation in Christ, if any consolation of love, if any fellowship of the Spirit, if any tender mercies and compassions,**

Paul begins the most weighty section of the Epistle with an impassioned appeal for unity based on the Christian experience of his readers [vv 1–4]. The repeated 'if' which

[39]

introduces this fourfold appeal does not express doubt, but rather assumes a condition of reality ('if . . . as is in fact the case'), and thus has the force of an affirmative statement. 'The four clauses seem to be arranged in pairs, one relating to union with Christ and its benefit, the other to communion with the Spirit and its benefit' (Plummer).

If there is therefore any exhortation in Christ, As sharers in Christ's life, the Philippians are under an obligation to heed the exhortation of Christ's apostle to work together in harmony [cf I *Cor* 1.10]. For all who are 'in Christ' are subject to the *rule* of Christ, and must therefore so listen to the *word* of Christ that they may never behave in a way which is contrary to the *mind* of Christ [*v* 5].

if there is any solace afforded by love, (Arndt-Gingrich) The second appeal is based on the comfort which they have found in Christ's love, for only an experience of *his* love has the constraining power to silence all disputing and to promote the true spirit of concord between believers [*v* 14].

if any fellowship with the Spirit, (NIV) Or 'any participation in the Spirit' (RSV). As believers in Christ they are all sharers in the same Spirit, who has made them fellow-members of the one body [I *Cor* 12.13]. This appeal to their spiritual experience is clearly intended to underline the inconsistency of indulging in that spirit of self-assertion which fosters divisions within the church [*vv* 3, 4]. They must rather seek 'to keep the unity of the Spirit in the bond of peace' [*Eph* 4.3].

if any tender mercies and compassions, The ground of the final appeal is found in the feelings of affection and sympathy which the Spirit himself inspires. If they now show such tenderness toward one another and forget their differences, they will make Paul's joy complete [v 2]. 'Chrysostom calls attention to the intense earnestness of these four clauses. The need for unity is so great that exhortation has become entreaty' (Plummer).

*V*2: **make full my joy, that ye be of the same mind, having the same love, being of one accord, of one mind;**

Although Paul is glad that he can base his appeal to the Philippians on what he knows are the realities of their spiritual experience, his cup of joy will be filled to the brim only if they respond to his urgent call for unity by being 'of the same mind'. The importance of the verb in Paul's argument can be gauged from the fact that no less than 10 of its 23 occurrences in his writings are found in this Epistle. True spiritual unity, as opposed to mere outward uniformity, depends upon a holy unanimity of thought. Christianity is first and foremost a condition of mind. Hence they cannot work together harmoniously unless they share the same disposition. Paul next shows how this 'thinking the same thing' must work itself out in the life of the church. First, it involves 'having the same love' for one another, as befits those who are loved by the same Saviour and who share the same Spirit [v 1]. Secondly, it means 'being of one accord, of one mind'. These are to be taken together as providing a '*more precise definition* of the previously mentioned unity of mind: *with harmony of soul cherishing the one sentiment*' (H. A. W. Meyer). As the inner motivation is the mainspring of all activity, the community of believers must share the same feeling if they are to work together in the same cause. Churches are so often upset by people with 'personality problems' that the very idea of working together may seem like an impossible ideal. Such difficulties can be resolved, but only by the way of lowliness which was exemplified by the Lord himself [*vv* 3–5; cf 4.2].

*V*3: *doing* nothing through faction or through vainglory, but in lowliness of mind each counting other better than himself;

Paul here diagnoses the malaise of the church and points to its remedy. It is clear from 3.12–16 that some were claiming to have already attained spiritual perfection, but to claim a 'glory' belonging to the *future* state was a form of '*vain*glory' that threatened to destroy the fellowship by the party-spirit and jealousy which it introduced (so J-F Collange). Such overweening pride is, alas, the most marked feature of those who are convinced of their own perfection. 'Egotism and boastfulness were apparently the perils besetting the Philippian Church . . . It is a strange phenomenon in religious history that intense earnestness so frequently breeds a spirit mingled of censoriousness and conceit' (Kennedy). Paul offers no palliative for this dire condition, but a radical cure which reaches to the very root of the disease. They must cultivate the lowliness of mind that counts others better than themselves. The Greek moralists despised humility because they regarded it as a form of servile subjection which was at odds with their concept of freedom. But Jesus exploded this false idea of human autonomy by living in perfect obedience to the Father's will [*vv* 5–8]. For in thus subjecting himself to God, he became the servant of all, and thereby provided the pattern for all authentic service [*Mark* 10.45; *Luke* 22.37]. As Jesus

[42]

brought this new spirit into the world, so his disciples must be imbued with the same lowliness of mind [*v* 5]. In the case of the sinless Jesus, this humility stemmed from his sense of entire dependence upon God as man; whereas in our case, it also springs from the sense of our own sinfulness before God (cf Trench, *Synonyms* p. 141). Perfectionism ministers to pride because it eradicates the sense of sin, but a high regard for self is impossible in those who are convinced of their sinful failings. 'Humility dispels the self-importance which is continually taking and asserting the measure of its own claims, when it comes into contact with others . . . Every man that knows his own heart finds, and must find, much in it to give him a low estimate of himself, and he cannot tell what graces may be cherished in the bosoms of those around him; they may be superior to his own. Nor has he any cause to be vain of any gifts conferred on him – "Who maketh thee to differ?" The original gift, and the impulse to cultivate it, are alike from above . . . But where there is self-assertion or rivalry to secure the "chief seat" and win applause, then the impulses of such vanity necessarily create alienation and disorder' (Eadie).

*V*4: **not looking each of you to his own things, but each of you also to the things of others.**

This admonition is especially relevant to our day when so many seem to imagine that Christianity consists in 'doing one's own thing', of following one's own spiritual bent, without respect to the welfare of one's fellow-members in the body of Christ. But to exhibit such a concern with 'number one' is to bring the values of the world into the church. Christ has a care for the weakest in his flock as well as for those who believe themselves to be the strongest!

[43]

What Paul means is well conveyed by Lenski: 'Look to the spiritual interests of others, then also to your own. Do this, all of you, each one'. As Eadie aptly remarks, 'It is not myself alone or in isolation, as if others did not exist, but myself with them and they with me, in earnest brotherhood and love. My object must not be simply to outstrip them in religious attainment, but to bring them and myself to a higher stage of Christian excellence'.

V 5: **Have this mind in you, which was also in Christ Jesus:**

Adopt towards one another the same attitude which (was**) also (**found**) in Christ Jesus,** (C. F. D. Moule) Paul now presses home his call for humility by appealing to Christ as the supreme example of self-sacrificing love. 'It is the spirit which animated our Lord in the act of His incarnation which His apostle would see us imitate. He would have us in all our acts to be like Christ, as He showed Himself to be in the innermost core of His being, when He became poor, He that was rich, that we by His poverty might be made rich . . . If we would follow Christ, we must, every one of us, not in pride but in humility, yet not in lowness but in lowliness, not degrade ourselves but forget ourselves, and seek every man not his own things but those of others . . . Our self-abnegation is thus not for our own sake, but for the sake of others. And thus it is not to mere self-denial that Christ calls us, but specifically to self-sacrifice: not to unselfing ourselves, but to unselfishing ourselves. Self-denial for its own sake is in its very nature ascetic, monkish. It concentrates our whole attention on self-knowledge, self-control – and can therefore eventuate in nothing other than the very apotheosis of selfishness . . .

It is not to this that Christ's example calls us. He did not cultivate self, even His divine self: He took no account of self . . . He was led by His love for others into the world, to forget Himself in the needs of others, to sacrifice self once for all upon the altar of sympathy. Self-sacrifice brought Christ into the world. And self-sacrifice will lead us, His followers, not away from but into the midst of men' (B. B. Warfield, 'Imitating the Incarnation', *The Saviour of the World*, pp. 167–183). It should be noted that the appeal here is to the church as a community and not merely to isolated individuals. There is such a thing as the sanctification of the congregation as well as of the individual believer.

*V*6: **who, existing in the form of God, counted not the being on an equality with God a thing to be grasped, 7 but emptied himself, taking the form of a servant, being made in the likeness of men; 8 and being found in fashion as a man, he humbled himself, becoming obedient *even* unto death, yea, the death of the cross. 9 Wherefore also God highly exalted him, and gave unto him the name which is above every name; 10 that in the name of Jesus every knee should bow, of *things* in heaven and *things* on earth and *things* under the earth, 11 and that every tongue should confess that Jesus Christ is Lord, to the glory of God the Father.**

As a result of recent study, this majestic passage is now generally regarded as a 'hymn to Christ' of pre-Pauline origin, but the possibility that Paul here incorporates an earlier composition of his own should not be lightly dismissed. In a spirited defence of the apostolic authorship, E. F. Scott points out that Paul's poetic gift is amply demonstrated in many 'splendid outbursts' in his Epistles [cf 1 Cor 13]. According to E. Stauffer, the passage is one of Paul's characteristic incarnation formulas, for he finds the same 'descent-ascent' motif worked into *Rom* 10.6ff and concludes that Paul is quoting a 'credal hymn' which he composed at an earlier date. As the hymn is both from the literary and theological point of view 'the work of a master', J-F Collange thinks that to deny the authorship to the apostle would be ungracious. More forthright is the judgment of W. G. Kümmel who states that 'nothing compels the conclusion that Paul himself could not have formulated this hymn' (*Introduction to the New Testament*, p. 335). No one today would care to dispute Paul's immense debt to those who were 'in Christ' before him, but in taking over this 'traditional' material he always stamped his personality upon it and made it indisputably his own. It is therefore safer to accept the whole hymn as Paul's rather than to suggest with E. Lohmeyer that those elements which break its metrical symmetry are Pauline additions, for at present we have no means of proving the authenticity of such proposed reconstructions of the hymn.[1]

who, existing in the form of God, Of the many different interpretations of this notoriously difficult passage, the classic view which takes 'form of God' in a metaphysical sense still seems to be the most fruitful, especially since modern Christology proceeds on the highly questionable assumption that the New Testament statements about Christ are a purely 'functional' account of his saving acts. Here the imperfect participle, 'existing', in contrast to the following aorists, refers to Christ's pre-existent state and 'points to indefinite continuance of being' (J. Gwynn). As

1. G. B. Caird provides an interesting critique of Lohmeyer's influential thesis in *Paul's Letters from Prison*, pp. 100–104.

the word 'form' was used to denote the essence of a thing, John Murray maintains that 'the form of God' does not mean anything less than Godhood. 'The accent falls upon the fulness of his Godhood, upon his being originally, natively, essentially God in the full possession of all that is distinctive of God in his majesty and glory. This is the dignity of his divine identity, the dignity of unabridged Deity' ('The Mystery of Godliness', *Collected Writings of John Murray*, Vol. 3, p. 237).[2]

did not count his existence-in-a-manner-equal-to-God something to cling to, (Hendriksen) This focuses upon the humiliation which was involved in Christ's pre-incarnate decision not to cling to his divine 'existential glory, the majesty of his revelation, the greatness and splendour of his manner of being' (S. Greijdanus cited by J. J. Müller). As Paul reminded the Corinthians of this great act of renunciation to encourage their generosity [2 *Cor* 8.9], so he administers an implicit rebuke to the quarrelling Philippians by showing them that Christ did not insist upon his rights but in love willingly waived them that he might save the lost [*vv* 7, 8]. Thus an overriding pastoral purpose ensures that there is no separation of theology and ethics in Paul. He never teaches doctrine for its own sake. His highest theological flights are always related to the down-to-earth problems of Christian living.

but emptied himself, taking the form of a servant, But instead of appearing 'in the form of God', Christ emptied himself by taking 'the form of a servant'. It is not

2. For a further fine discussion, see B. B. Warfield, 'The Person of Christ According to the New Testament', *Biblical Doctrines*, pp. 176–182, and *The Person and Work of Christ*, pp. 38–44.

said that Christ 'emptied' (*ekenōsen*) himself of his essential equality with God, or of his divine attributes, as is falsely inferred by the proponents of the modern 'kenotic' theory, which has been aptly described by E. Digges La Touche as 'incarnation by divine suicide' (cited by L. Berkhof in *The History of Christian Doctrines*, p. 121). 'Emptied' is here used metaphorically to underline the contrast between the pre-incarnate glory and the incarnate humiliation: 'to show that Christ utterly renounced and laid aside the majesty which he possessed in his original state. Its most satisfactory definition is found in the succeeding details which describe the incidents of Christ's humanity, and with these exegesis is compelled to stop. The word does not indicate a surrender of deity, nor a paralysis of deity, nor a change of personality, nor a break in the continuity of self-consciousness. Christ's consciousness of deity was not suspended during his earthly life' (Vincent, *ICC*, p. 89). 'Emptied' therefore means that Christ veiled his glory when he 'stripped himself of the insignia of majesty' (Lightfoot). But paradoxically, Christ emptied himself *by taking* (the aorist participle denotes coincident action) the form of a servant, i.e. by an *addition* rather than a subtraction. 'He took the form of a servant while he retained the form of God! It is exactly that which makes our salvation possible and achieves it' (Hendriksen). Yet though Christ remained essentially one with the Father [*John* 10.30], the stark reality of his servanthood necessarily involved complete subordination to the Father's will, so that he refused every temptation to make independent use of his divine powers during the period of his humiliation [*John* 14.10, 28]. This taking the form of a servant also made Christ subject to the law of God in both its active and passive demands [*Gal* 4.4, 5]. He came to fulfil all its precepts as our representative, and to exhaust its penalty as our sin-bearing substitute. 'To have taken the form of a servant in reference to any human will or authority would have contradicted his dignity and mission. It was to God the Father that he assumed this relation and it was to the will of the Father that he surrendered himself in the fulness of subjection and obligation' (John Murray) [cf *John* 6.38; 17.4].

being made in the likeness of men; As to the manner of Christ's appearing, he was a real man among men, but Paul uses the word 'likeness' to show that in assuming our humanity (sin alone excepted: cf *Rom* 8.3) he did not cease to be himself – the eternal Son of God. So though Christ entered upon a genuinely human existence at a definite point in time, his prior existence 'in the form of God' means that the secret of his person cannot be penetrated by those who think of him in merely human terms [*Matt* 16.16f].

and being found in fashion as a man, This marks an advance on the previous clause. Having become man, Christ was recognized as such by those who saw him 'in the days of his flesh' [*Heb* 5.7]. The word 'fashion' refers to his external appearance, so that here the contrast 'is between what He *is* in himself, and what He *appeared* in the eyes of men' (Lightfoot). The majority did not see beyond the outward guise, and this failure to perceive his divine dignity meant that his whole earthly walk was one long *via dolorosa* which led inevitably to the cross [cf *Is* 53.2, 3].

he humbled himself, becoming obedient *even* unto death, First, the pre-incarnate Christ emptied himself *by* taking the form of a servant (v 7). Then having become man, he humbled himself *by* becoming obedient even up to the point of death. The description covers Christ's entire life upon earth, and shows that his undeviating subjection to the Father's will led him to accept a life of humiliation which culminated in his death. 'This extreme height reached by His obedience was, however, just the extreme *depth* of the humiliation, and thereby at the same time its *end*' (Meyer).

yea, the death of the cross. The climax is in the word 'cross', and it must have deeply impressed those whose citizenship made them exempt from that hideous form of capital punishment which was reserved for slaves and foreigners. 'Far be the very name of the cross, not only from the body, but even from the thought, the eyes, the ears of Roman citizens' (Cicero). Yet for Christ the greatest anguish of the cross consisted not in the awful physical agony, but in the abyss of spiritual dereliction he experienced as he bore our sin [*Matt* 27.46; *Gal* 3.13]. 'He humbled himself to the accursed death of the cross. There were no lower depths possible, for the cross bespeaks the whole curse of God upon sin. It is humiliation inimitable, unrepeated, unrepeatable' (John Murray).

Wherefore also God highly exalted him, and gave unto him the name which is above every name; This is the turning point in the great drama of redemption. In the first part of the 'hymn' attention has been focused on the self-humbling of Christ, but now God takes the initiative by advancing Christ to the place of highest honour. As the reward for Christ's obedience unto death, God highly exalted him, and graciously gave to him the name which is above every name. 'Even Christ receives the recompense as God's *gift of grace*, and hence also He *prays* Him for it, John 17.5. The glory of the *exaltation* did not stand to that possessed *before the incarnation* in the relation of a *plus*, but it affected the *entire divine-human* person, that entered on the *regnum gloriae*' (Meyer). 'The name which is above every name' can only be the name 'Lord' (*Kyrios*, v 11), which is the word used in the Greek version of the Old Testament to render the ineffable name of God, the tetragrammaton YHWH. 'He hath changed the ineffable name into a name utterable by man, and desirable by all the world; the majesty is all arrayed in robes of mercy, the tetragrammaton or adorable mystery of the patriarchs is made fit for pronunciation and expression when it becometh the name of the Lord's Christ' (Jeremy Taylor cited by Kennedy).

that in the name of Jesus every knee should bow, of *things* **in heaven and** *things* **on earth and** *things* **under the earth,** This expresses the purpose of the exaltation. In adapting the words of *Is* 45.23 for his purpose [cf *Rom* 14.11], Paul here transfers to Christ the universal homage which is there claimed by God. As Eadie says, 'In the name of Jesus' means 'in recognition of it, or of the authority and majesty of Him who bears it. . . . If beings bow in recognition of the name of Jesus, it is to Jesus Himself as bearing such a name, that they offer homage'. Paul's threefold classification is comprehensive in its scope, and shows that there is no sphere within the created order which is exempt from Christ's universal lordship. Although the ASV supplies 'things' to make up the sense, the neuter is clearly inappropriate in a passage which speaks of bowing the knee and confessing with the tongue (v 11). What the apostle has in view is the future submission of all intelligent beings before Christ, whether by choice or by compulsion. 'The first are all the blessed angels and the saints in heaven; the second are all the men on earth; the third are all the demons and the damned in hell. The three groups include all created personal beings. All shall bow in submission and make this acknowledgment or confession with either joy and bliss or dismay' (Lenski).

and that every tongue should confess that Jesus Christ is Lord, In affirming that 'Jesus Christ is Lord', Paul is echoing the earliest creed of the Christian church [cf *Rom* 10.9; 1 *Cor* 12.3]. This confession of the present Lordship of Christ which is already made within the context of the church's worship thus anticipates the universal recognition that will follow at the parousia. 'Paul has the exalted Jesus in mind in thus speaking of Him. It was only on His exaltation that Jesus entered upon His dominion. But it by no means follows that he conceived Jesus to have acquired His "Lordship", in the sense of His inherent right to reign, by His exaltation . . . That he recognized that this Jesus had entered upon the actual exercise of His universal dominion only on His resurrection and ascension, and in this sense had received it as a reward for His work on earth [*Phil* 2.9; *Rom* 14.9] merely means that, no less than to our Lord Himself, the earthly manifestation of Jesus was to Paul an estate of humiliation upon which glory followed. But the glory which thus followed the humiliation was to Paul, too, a glory which belonged of right to Jesus, to whom His lowly life on earth, not His subsequent exaltation, was a strange experience' (B. B. Warfield, *The Lord of Glory*, pp. 223–225).

to the glory of God the Father. Paul fittingly concludes with a doxology expressing the *ultimate* purpose of Christ's exaltation [vv 9–11]. 'Christ as God has the right to the adoration of the universe, but as God-man He has for His special service received a special investiture. He could not be worshipped at all, if He were not God, and He is now worshipped on this peculiar ground, because He has done and suffered as the apostle tells us. But the prime place is occupied by God the Father, to whom service was rendered by Christ, while the success of such service and its consequent reward by Him are a source of glory to Him. In the honour paid to His exalted Son, His own character is more fully seen and admired' (Eadie).

*V*12: **So then, my beloved, even as ye have always obeyed, not as in my presence only, but now much more in my absence, work out your own salvation with fear and trembling;**

Having reminded his readers of the exemplary self-sacrifice of Christ, Paul now proceeds to point out its practical bearing upon the life of the church as a whole, thus resuming his appeal to them to show the same lowliness of mind towards one another [vv 1–5]. Hence he is not exhorting them as individuals to work out their personal salvation. He is rather urging them to forsake self-assertive zeal, so that they can all work together for the spiritual health of the whole church as a witnessing community [v 14ff]. For a church torn by strife never makes a favourable impact upon the world! With his own approaching departure in view, Paul seems to have modelled his charge upon Moses' farewell address [*Deut* 32.1–5]. But whereas Moses rebukes the children of Israel for their past disobedience, Paul believes that he can count upon the Philippians' obedience to the gospel even in his absence, because God is present with them in the power of his enabling grace [v 13]. At first sight this confidence hardly seems compatible with a feeling of 'fear and trembling', but the other occasions on which Paul used this expression indicate a manward rather than a Godward reference (cf 1 *Cor* 2.3; 2 *Cor* 7.15; *Eph* 6.5]. The phrase denotes an attitude of humility in relationship to other men. 'What Paul here demands of the Church is the same humility he called for in verse 3, the same willingness to see something from another's point of view . . . The man who approaches another within the congregation with fear and trembling acknowledges that he has submitted his own life to the power of God and that all vindication proceeds from God alone [1.28]' (W. L. Lane).

*V*13: **for it is God who worketh in you both to will and to work, for his good pleasure.**

for it is God who works effectively among you, The Philippians do not need to wait for Paul's arrival to reform the flaws in their fellowship, because God himself is effectively at work in their midst (so Collange). As God thus bestows both the power to will and to work, in order to fulfil his good pleasure in restoring the divided community to full spiritual health, it is clear that no room is left for any boasting in human achievement [*Is* 26.12]. 'This shows how empty is the presumption of those who divide the glory of our course in the faith between God and ourselves; freely granting that God works in them the beginnings of salvation, but pretending that, after having received the first tokens of His grace, they are afterwards the authors of the rest, which they express by a word full of vanity, saying that they co-operate with God, making themselves, by these means, companions of the Godhead in this work. The apostle here throws down all this project of their pride, pronouncing, gloriously, that *it is God which works in them to will and to do*, the progress and the end, as well as the beginning' (Daillé).

*V*14: **Do all things without murmurings and questionings;**

'All things' stands at the beginning in the Greek text to emphasize the importance of doing everything in the right spirit. Paul's injunction plainly refers to the internal dissension which was disturbing the peace of the church. Perhaps the two terms are used to indicate cause and effect, for a spirit of grumbling discontent usually leads to ill-natured wrangling. The word 'murmurings' recalls the rebellious complaints of the Israelites against God [1 *Cor* 10.10], but as the Philippians are clearly not guilty of such presumption, Paul must be alluding to their grumbling amongst themselves. The second term, 'questionings' or disputings, may point to arguments provoked by doctrinal differences. We know that there were some at Philippi who imagined that they had already attained spiritual perfection [cf 3.12]. As such people are not noticeably meek in advancing their claims to superior holiness, this attitude of self-assertion would naturally be challenged by the 'ordinary' Christians in the church, and the ensuing arguments would tend to divide the fellowship into opposing camps. This is only a tentative suggestion, because it is obviously impossible for us now to determine the precise situation Paul had in view. But his condemnation of the complaining and arguing that so frequently mars the relationship between believers is certainly not open to question.

V15: that ye may become blameless and harmless, children of God without blemish in the midst of a crooked and perverse generation, among whom ye are seen as lights in the world,

The Philippians must avoid all unholy strife [v 14], in order that they may become the kind of people whose witness will commend itself to outsiders. Paul is here drawing their attention to the vital importance of consistent Christian living, for though God entrusts the treasure of the gospel to frail earthen vessels, the vessels must be clean if their witness is to be effective [2 Cor 4.7]. 'Blameless' not only requires purity of life, but also demands that it may be so evident to all, that no charge can be justly levelled against the witnessing community. 'Harmless' literally means 'unmixed', and indicates that which is free of foreign additions, as of wine unmixed with water or of metal without any alloy in it. The word thus points to a purity which is not contaminated by any foreign element that would alter the character of the church and make void its testimony to the truth. So they must unitedly strive to become 'children of God without blemish', by living up to the privileges which are now theirs by the adoption of grace [Gal 3.26], for it is only when the church is demonstrably different from its pagan environment that any impression is made upon 'a crooked and perverse generation' [cf Matt 5.13–16]. The latter phrase was part of Moses' accusation against the erring Israelites [Deut 32.5], but Paul applies it to the sinful world of moral darkness in which his readers 'shine like stars in the universe' (NIV). Because they are illuminated by the light of Christ, they are able to reflect that light for the guidance of others, just as the sailor plots his course by the stars.

V 16: **holding forth the word of life; that I may have whereof to glory in the day of Christ, that I did not run in vain neither labour in vain.**

This further defines the function of the Philippians as luminaries in a sin-darkened world [v 15]. It is their missionary rôle to hold forth 'the word of life', i.e. the gospel which alone has the power to bring life to the spiritually dead. 'As they made known its doctrines, and impressed men with a sense of its importance, as their actions, in their purity and harmony, exhibited its life and power, did they hold it forth' (Eadie). Paul urges them to remain faithful to the substance and spirit of the gospel, so that on the day of Christ he may be able to glory in the fact that he did not run or labour in vain. Both metaphors emphasize the energy expended in the fulfilment of his apostolic commission. 'This, then, was a sly goad to stir up the Philippians to constancy and perseverance in the faith; as if he said, Act in such a manner that I may rejoice and glory in your piety, not here only, where every thing is changeable, but also in the great day of Christ; that the good beginnings which I have seen and still see among you may be persevered in and crowned with constancy; that time may cause no change in them, if it be not for the better; so that when the Lord shall appear, after our combats are ended, I may then also have cause to say with joy, to your glory and mine, that I have not laboured in vain' (Daillé).

*V*17: **Yea, and if I am offered upon the sacrifice and service of your faith, I joy, and rejoice with you all: 18 and in the same manner do ye also joy, and rejoice with me.**

In facing the real possibility of imminent martyrdom, Paul humbly compares his death to a drink-offering that is poured out as the accompanying libation to the sacrificial offering of the Philippians' faith, which is proved genuine by their own willingness to suffer for the gospel [1.29, 30]. It is because Paul knows that his friends are united with him in the great work of advancing the cause of Christ in the world that he can greet even the prospect of death with undaunted joy. So from his grim prison in Rome he rejoices with them all, and bids them also to rejoice with him. Paul here piles up the terms to express his joy under the most adverse circumstances, because he clearly expects his fellow-sufferers at Philippi to meet their trials in the same spirit. And he further puts them on their mettle by using a metaphor which depicts his own suffering as an auxiliary part of the sacrifice made by them. As Lightfoot well says, The apostle's 'language expresses the fundamental idea of the Christian Church, in which an universal priesthood has supplanted the exclusive ministrations of a select tribe or class: see 1 *Pet* 2.5, *a holy priesthood to offer up spiritual sacrifices.* The Philippians are the priests; their faith (or their good works springing from their faith) is the sacrifice: St Paul's life-blood the accompanying libation. Commentators have much confused the image by representing St Paul himself as the sacrificer'.

*V*19: **But I hope in the Lord Jesus to send Timothy**

shortly unto you, that I also may be of good comfort, when I know your state.

Paul now acquaints the Philippians with what he has planned for their benefit [vv 19–30]. He is sending this letter with Epaphroditus without waiting for the result of the trial [v 25], but as soon as the case is decided Timothy will follow with the news [v 23]. Although Paul is quite prepared for an unfavourable verdict [v 17], he still hopes to be acquitted and released for further service [v 24].

But I hope in the Lord Jesus to send Timothy shortly unto you, Paul often uses the verb 'hope' in formulating his travel plans [*Rom* 15.24; 1 *Cor* 16.7; *Philemon* 22], and this verse shows that all his plans are made in the full consciousness of his union with the Lord Jesus and in humble dependence upon what is his will for him. 'The Christian is a part of Christ, a member of His body. His every thought and word and deed proceeds from Christ, as the centre of volition. Thus he loves in the Lord, he hopes in the Lord, he boasts in the Lord, he labours in the Lord, etc. He has one guiding principle in acting and in forbearing to act, *only in the Lord* [1 *Cor* 7.39]' (Lightfoot).

that I also may be of good comfort, when I know your state. R. P. Martin helpfully clarifies the force of this 'also': 'not only will you be encouraged to have first-hand news of me here, I too shall be heartened when I get news of you at Philippi on Timothy's return'. This means that the main object of Timothy's mission would be to exercise such a ministry in their midst that he would be able to comfort Paul with the report that unity had been restored [1.27].

[59]

*V*20: **For I have no man likeminded, who will care truly for your state.**

I have no one like him, who will be genuinely anxious for your welfare. (RSV) Paul is not comparing Timothy with himself (for which he would have written: 'I have no one *else* like myself'), but with others who have no real concern for the welfare of his friends at Philippi [v 21]. Timothy was unique because only he shared Paul's anxious solicitude for the churches [2 *Cor* 11.28]. 'There is a right and a wrong anxiety, just as a right and a wrong attention to one's own interests [v 4]' (Plummer). As Paul's most trusted assistant, Timothy has the best interests of the Philippians at heart, and he is both competent and willing to serve them without regard to the cost to himself. 'Timothy was of a choice and excellent spirit that naturally cared for the Churches' welfare; few such now-a-days' (Trapp).

*V*21: **For they all seek their own, not the things of Jesus Christ.**

Of the other Christians who might have been entrusted with this important mission to Philippi, Paul sadly records that none was willing to undertake such an onerous task, for they all put their own interests before those of Jesus Christ. Although this reflects no credit on those whom Paul charitably refuses to name, it highlights the self-sacrifice of Timothy, whose single-minded devotion to Christ's cause is demonstrated by his care for the Philippians. 'It may seem at first sight as if it were no great fault to seek one's own; but how insufferable it is in the servants of Christ appears from the fact that it renders those whom it possesses utterly useless. For it is impossible that he who is devoted to self, should spend himself for the Church. Then, you will say, did Paul cultivate men who were worthless and pretenders? I answer that it is not to be understood as if they had been intent only on their own interests, and had no care whatever for the Church, but that, involved in their own private affairs, they were the more negligent to promote the public advantage of the Church. For it must necessarily be, that one or other of two dispositions rules in us: either that, overlooking ourselves, we are devoted to Christ and the things that are Christ's, or that, too intent on our own advantage, we serve Christ perfunctorily' (John Calvin).

*V*22: **But ye know the proof of him, that, as a child *serveth* a father, *so* he served with me in furtherance of the gospel.**

But (Timothy's) proven worth you know, In contrast to such self-seeking, Timothy had given the Philippians first-hand proof of his worth, just as metals are approved by testing [cf *Acts* 16.3; 19.22; 20.3–6]. 'They were no strangers to his excellence – it had been tested during previous visits' (Eadie).

how as a child (to) a father, he served with me in the furtherance of the gospel, 'The slight want of correspondence between the two parts of the sentence, reflects accurately the twofold relation between the men. To *one another*, they were "as child *to* father"; to *God*, they were alike servants, one "serving *with*" the other' (Gwynn).

*V*23: **Him therefore I hope to send forthwith, so soon**

as I shall see how it will go with me: 24 but I trust in the Lord that I myself also shall come shortly.

This trusted minister of the gospel is therefore the man whom Paul will send to Philippi as soon as the outcome of his trial is known. Then Timothy will bring the news of Paul's condemnation or release. But Paul's trust in the Lord is such that he also expects to visit them shortly [1.25]. We know from the evidence furnished by the Pastoral Epistles that Paul's first trial resulted in his release, and that he enjoyed a further period of useful service before his final imprisonment and death in Rome (c AD 67).

*V*25: **But I counted it necessary to send to you Epaphroditus, my brother and fellow-worker and fellow-soldier, and your messenger and minister to my need;**

But I think it is necessary to send back to you Epaphroditus, (NIV) Paul next explains his reasons for sending back Epaphroditus with this letter [*vv* 25–30]. Epaphroditus, whose name means 'charming', is not to be identified with the Epaphras mentioned in *Col* 1.7, 4.12, and we know nothing more of him than Paul tells us here. In Paul's glowing commendation of this dedicated servant of Christ, the first three terms describe his relation to the apostle, and the final pair his attachment to the Philippians.

my brother and fellow-worker and fellow-soldier, 'My brother in the faith, my fellow-worker in preaching, my fellow-soldier in adversity' (Anselm). Lightfoot points out that the three words are arranged in an ascending scale: 'common sympathy, common work, common danger and toil and suffering'.

and your messenger and minister to my need; As the
'apostle' or appointed delegate of the Philippian church [cf
2 *Cor* 8.23], Epaphroditus was sent to perform a sacrificial
service for Paul by presenting their gift of money [4.18]
and ministering to his needs in prison on their behalf [*v*
30].

*V*26: **since he longed after you all, and was sore
troubled, because ye had heard that he was sick:**

**for he has been longing for you all, and has been
distressed because you heard that he was ill.** (RSV) This
states why Paul has decided to send back Epaphroditus at
once. It is unlikely that Epaphroditus would have travelled
alone to Rome, especially when he was bringing a sum of
money to Paul. So if he became ill shortly after their arrival,
his companions would take back the unwelcome news on
their return to Philippi. This illness naturally intensified his
longing to see all his brethren at home, and he was also
greatly distressed to realize that news of his condition
would have filled them with grief.

*V*27: **for indeed he was sick nigh unto death: but God
had mercy on him; and not on him only, but on me
also, that I might not have sorrow upon sorrow.**

Paul here movingly reveals his own reaction to Epaphroditus' illness, which was so serious that he nearly died. But
despite his anxiety for the life of his friend, Paul did not
heal him by exercising 'the signs of an apostle' [2 *Cor*
12.12], because 'even in that charismatic era the apostles
could not perform miracles whenever they felt so inclined.
Their will was subject to *God's* will' (Hendriksen). But in

graciously restoring Epaphroditus, God showed mercy both to him and to Paul, who was thus spared from being overwhelmed by 'sorrow upon sorrow'. As Eadie says, The sorrow which he already possessed was not the sickness of Epaphroditus, 'for even after his convalescence, he speaks of himself as only lightened in sorrow, but not entirely freed from it. A sorrow would still remain after Epaphroditus had departed, as is intimated in the next verse, the sorrow produced by his present situation – his captivity and all its embarrassments. This statement is in no way inconsistent with what he had written in 1.20, etc, for his condition is there looked at from a very different point of view'.

*V*28: **I have sent him therefore the more diligently, that, when ye see him again, ye may rejoice, and that I may be the less sorrowful.**

Accordingly, I am sending him (back) the more eagerly in order that when you see him again you may rejoice and I may be less sorrowful. (Hendriksen) The Philippians had intended that Epaphroditus should stay with Paul and attend to his needs in prison, but circumstances alter cases [*vv* 26, 27], and Paul now deems it best to send back their brother so that they may rejoice in his safe return. By sharing in the joy of this reunion Paul's sorrow will be lessened. 'The original sorrow, which still remains his portion, will be lessened by sympathy with the Philippians' joy at having Epaphroditus home again and in good health' (Plummer).

*V*29: **Receive him therefore in the Lord with all joy; and hold such in honour: 30 because for the work of**

Christ he came nigh unto death, hazarding his life to supply that which was lacking in your service toward me.

Having explained why Epaphroditus is returning earlier than anticipated, Paul now plainly bids the Philippians to give him the welcome he deserves. As he was sent so that they might rejoice [*v* 28], they must therefore receive him 'in the Lord' with all joy, for such men are to be honoured and prized.

because he almost died for the work of Christ, risking his life to make up for the help you could not give me. (NIV) Paul here gives the reason for valuing Epaphroditus so highly. The word translated as 'risking' really means that he gambled with his life by staking all in the service of Christ [cf *Rom* 16.4]. The noble example of Epaphroditus was followed by others, and certain laymen in the Early Church who risked their lives in caring for victims of the plague were known as 'the Gamblers'. 'That which was lacking in your service toward me' is an unfortunate rendering which suggests some neglect on the Philippians' part, and Paul's meaning is made much clearer by the NIV. 'The expression is complimentary and affectionate, to the effect that all that was wanting in the matter of their service was their ministration *in person*, which was supplied by Epaphroditus' (Vincent).

CHAPTER THREE

After a further call to rejoice in the Lord, Paul launches into a passionate warning against Judaizers whom he calls 'the mutilators', and shows that he had greater cause than they to trust in the righteousness of the law [vv 1–6]. But the privileges he once prized, he now counts as loss that he may gain Christ and his righteousness, and share in the resurrection from the dead [vv 7–11]. In contrast to the self-deluded who already claimed perfection, Paul still presses on toward the goal, and he enjoins the spiritually mature to strive after the same thing without losing hold of their present attainments [vv 12-16]. In presenting himself as an example to follow, Paul warns against the profligate professors whose god is their belly and who mind earthly things, whereas the true citizens of heaven eagerly await the return of Christ and the glory of the resurrection [vv 17–21].

V 1: **Finally, my brethren, rejoice in the Lord. To write the same things to you, to me indeed is not irksome, but for you it is safe.**

For the rest, my brothers, rejoice in the Lord. (Hendriksen) 'Finally' is rather misleading because it suggests that Paul is about to conclude the Epistle, whereas the expression is loosely used to introduce a new subject ('for the rest'). As the affectionate address 'my brothers' reminds

[66]

the Philippians of their glorious position as members of the same spiritual family, it serves to reinforce the renewed exhortation to rejoice [cf 2.18, 28], but this time Paul defines the sphere of this rejoicing by adding 'in the Lord'. The phrase points to the one ground of rejoicing and also excludes all confidence in the flesh [*v* 3]. Believers must indeed rejoice, but they can only do so 'in the Lord': only in union with him and relying solely upon his redemptive achievements on their behalf.

To write the same things to you is no trouble to me, and for you it is a safeguard. (Hendriksen) 'The same things' refers to the warning that follows and not to the call to rejoice. Although some suppose this relates to warnings given in previous letters which are lost, it is more likely that the earlier general warning to stand firm against the opponents of the gospel is here applied to the particular threat posed by the Judaizers [1.27-30]. As a faithful watchman for the souls of men, Paul is so diligent in repeating his warnings that he knows he is pure from the blood of all men [*Ezek* 33.2–6; *Acts* 20.26].

*V*2: **Beware of the dogs, beware of the evil workers, beware of the concision:**

The biting sarcasm of Paul's threefold indictment of the Judaizers is intended to ensure that if these emissaries of legalism make their way to Philippi they will be sent packing by the church.

Look out for the dogs, (RSV) As a term of reproach, the image suggested by this word was that of the diseased scavenger dogs which roamed about eastern cities, and it

[67]

thus signified for the Jew all that was impure and unclean [cf *Rev* 22.15]. Hence 'dogs' was the Jewish designation for all Gentiles, which Paul here hurls back at the Judaizers: *they* are the dogs, 'for they greedily devour the garbage of carnal ordinances' (Lightfoot).

look out for the evil-doers, (RSV) In their fanatical zeal, these pseudo-missionaries were engaged in the evil work of gaining converts from Gentile churches by corrupting the gospel of God's grace with the leaven of their legalism [cf *Matt* 23.15; 2 *Cor* 11.13–15]. 'Instead of *helping* the good cause, they actually *harm* it. They draw the attention away from Christ and his accomplished redemption, and fix it upon an outworn ritual, and upon human worth and attainment in insisting upon its perpetuation and application. Here is Satan's demolition crew. It is working very hard to demolish God's beautiful palace of grace and peace' (Hendriksen).

look out for those who mutilate the flesh. (RSV) Paul denies the honoured title of 'the circumcision' to the apostles of error and scathingly brands them as 'the mutilation'. Their circumcision was of no more value than the gashings of the prophets of Baal, 'because these men were circumcised merely *as regards the body*, and placed their confidence in this fleshly circumcision, but were wanting in the *inner, spiritual* circumcision, which that of the body typified [see v 3; *Rom* 2.28f; *Col* 2.11; *Eph* 2.11; *Acts* 7.51]. Comp *Gal* 5.11f. In the absence of this, their characteristic consisted simply in the bodily mutilation' (Meyer).

V 3: **for we are the circumcision, who worship by the**

Spirit of God, and glory in Christ Jesus, and have no confidence in the flesh:

Paul totally rejects the false claims of the Judaizers and roundly affirms: 'for *we* Christians are the circumcision, for their circumcision is only outward, whereas the *true* circumcision is that of the heart' [*Rom* 2.25–29; cf *Deut* 10.16; 30.6; *Jer* 4.4; *Ezek* 44.7]. In the three clauses that follow Paul sets forth the distinguishing characteristics of the true Israel of God [*Gal* 6.15, 16]. 'The notion that God even today recognizes two favoured groups – on the one hand the church and on the other the Jews – is thoroughly unscriptural' (Hendriksen). [Cf *John* 10.16].

who worship by the Spirit of God, To worship God acceptably requires an inward transformation by the Holy Spirit as the initiator of the New Covenant [*Jer* 31.31–34; *Ezek* 36.26f], and his enabling promotes that life of *service* which is the true *worship* [cf *Rom* 12.1, ASV margin]. 'Christians worship God through the Spirit of God. This is not to be restricted to prayer. It includes all that to which we are impelled by the Spirit. The Christian life fashioned by the Spirit is true *worship*' (H. Strathmann, *TDNT*, Vol IV, pp. 64–5).

and glory in Christ Jesus, This is our only boast! We glory in Christ Jesus 'as Him through whom alone we have attained righteousness, etc, see *v* 9; comp *Gal* 6.14' (Meyer). The verb used here is one of Paul's favourite and most characteristic words. 'It expresses with great vividness the high level of Christian life at which he is living: "exulting in Christ Jesus". It belongs to the same triumphant mood which finds utterance so often in this Epistle in *rejoice*. This victorious Christian gladness ought to sweep them past all earthly formalism and bondage to "beggarly elements" ' (Kennedy).

and have no confidence in the flesh: The 'flesh' is 'another name for external privilege, such as descent, and points to such merit as pride thinks due to formal obedience. It is a ground of confidence opposed to the righteousness of Christ – *v* 9' (Eadie).

V 4: **though I myself might have confidence even in the flesh: if any other man thinketh to have confidence in the flesh, I yet more:**

Paul here changes from 'we' to the emphatic 'I', as he recounts a vivid snatch of his spiritual autobiography. This is to show that his opposition to the Judaizers was not motivated by envy of their supposed advantages, since he had greater grounds for glorying on that score than they had themselves. So for the sake of argument, he 'places himself on the same standing ground with the Judaizers and, adopting their language, speaks of himself as having that which in fact he had renounced: comp 2 *Cor* 11.18 *since many glory according to the flesh, I will glory also*' (Lightfoot). Although Paul recognized the 'folly' of such boasting [2 *Cor* 11.17], it was necessary to list his Jewish credentials before showing that they were unable to provide the perfect righteousness God requires [*vv* 7–9]. He first lists the advantages which were his by birth [*v* 5], and then those which he later acquired by his own efforts [*vv* 5d, 6].

V 5: **circumcised the eighth day, of the stock of Israel, of the tribe of Benjamin, a Hebrew of Hebrews;**

The four advantages by birth are arranged in an ascending scale.

circumcised the eighth day, The first item in Paul's unimpeachable Jewish pedigree would be all the more impressive if some of the zealous Judaizers were only recently circumcised proselytes. 'Converts to Judaism were circumcised in maturity: Ishmaelites in their thirteenth year. He was thus shown to be neither a heathen nor an Ishmaelite' (Vincent). [*Gen* 17.9–14; *Lev* 12.3].

of the stock of Israel, One who was circumcised on the eighth day could still be the child of proselyte parents, but Paul belonged to the chosen race by direct descent. 'His parents were not grafted into the covenant people, but descended from the original stock' (Lightfoot).

of the tribe of Benjamin, Moreover, in a day when many Israelites had lost their tribal identity, Paul was proud to be a member of the tribe which gave Israel its first king, after whom he was doubtless named [*Acts* 13.21]. 'This tribe stood high in Jewish estimation, not only as descending from Rachel, Jacob's best-loved wife, but as remaining loyal to the house of David, and, after the exile, forming with Judah the foundation of the future nation' (Kennedy).

a Hebrew of Hebrews, Finally, Paul's racial purity was unspoilt by foreign influences. 'The expression implies characteristics of language and manners. He might be an Israelite and yet a child of Greek-speaking Jews: but his parents had retained their native tongue and customs, and he himself, while understanding and speaking Greek, also spoke in Hebrew on occasion. See *Acts* 21.40; 22.2' (Vincent).

V 5d: **as touching the law, a Pharisee; 6 as touching zeal, persecuting the church; as touching the righteousness which is in the law, found blameless.**

Paul's inherited privileges are followed by the three distinctions he had attained by his own choice and training.

as touching the law, a Pharisee; Although the Pharisees (or 'Separated Ones') fought a war on two fronts against the theological 'liberalism' of the Sadducees and the religious 'laxity' of the common people, they were the most influential party in Judaism and were generally respected for their piety (cf J. Jeremias, *Jerusalem in the Time of Jesus*, pp. 266–267). To join such a party was the natural choice for an all-or-nothing man like Saul of Tarsus, who studied the law under the famous Gamaliel at Jerusalem [*Acts* 22.3].

as touching zeal, persecuting the church; 'An expression of intense irony, condemning while he seems to exalt his former self' (Lightfoot). Paul thus recalls with shame his fanatical zeal in persecuting the church of Christ [*Gal* 1.13f], which is assailed when even one member of Christ's body is hurt [*Acts* 9.4f; 1 *Tim* 1.13]. But on his conversion, the persecutor became one of the persecuted [*Acts* 9.16]. 'He had persecuted, as the Jews are now persecuting him; and in each case the persecution was conscientious' (Plummer). [*Rom* 10.1–3].

as touching the righteousness which is in the law, found blameless. According to the Pharisaic understanding of what constituted obedience to the law, Paul was blameless in his scrupulous observance of all those minute duties imposed by a tradition intent upon attaining right-eousness by works [cf *v* 9]. A close parallel is furnished by the gospel story of the rich young man who claimed to have observed all the law's commands from his youth [*Mark* 10.20]. 'It was at the next step [*v* 7] that *he* stopped short. He was unable to "count all things loss for Christ" ' (Kennedy).

*V*7: **Howbeit what things were gain to me, these have I counted loss for Christ.**

Yet those things which I formerly reckoned to my credit I have come to count as loss for Christ's sake. (F. F. Bruce) Paul's confidence in the Judaistic method of reckoning up his fancied merits was shattered by his encounter with the Risen Christ on the road to Damascus. As his old life and all its cherished values collapsed around him, he realized that the things which he had prized as 'assets' were in fact 'liabilities', and so he bundled them all together and wrote them off as a complete loss. 'In the light of the all-transcending knowledge of Christ the life which trusts in, and appeals to, descent, the Law and achievement, is not just fruitless exertion but harmful in the absolute sense' (H. Schlier, *TDNT*, Vol III, p. 673).

*V*8: **Yea verily, and I count all things to be loss for the excellency of the knowledge of Christ Jesus my Lord: for whom I suffered the loss of all things, and do count them but refuse,**

Yes, what is more, I certainly do count all things to be

sheer loss because of the all-surpassing excellence of knowing Christ Jesus my Lord, (Hendriksen) In addition to the things just mentioned, Paul continues to count *all* things as sheer loss because of the infinitely more valuable gain of knowing 'Christ Jesus my Lord'. As the emphatic fulness of the designation points to the supreme worthiness of the One who is the object of this knowledge, so the warmth with which Paul claims him as '*my* Lord' shows that his knowledge is not based on hearsay but personal communion. Paul at last attained the true 'knowledge of God' when he came to know the Son who had so fully revealed the Father's great love. This knowledge 'is directly connected with the surrender of the soul to Christ, but, as Paul teaches, that always means a close intimacy with Him, from which there springs an ever-growing knowledge of His spirit and will. Such knowledge lays a stable foundation for the Christian character, preventing it from evaporating into a mere unreasoning emotionalism' (Kennedy). [Cf *Eph* 1.17, 18; 3.19; *Col* 1.9, 10; 2.2, 3; 3.10].

for whom I suffered the loss of all things, 'These emphatic words suit the mouth of one who had been disowned by his family, and reduced from a position of wealth and influence in his nation to poverty and contempt' (W. M. Ramsay, *St. Paul the Traveller and the Roman Citizen*, p. 36).

and do count them but refuse, Paul expresses his utter revulsion at the attempts of the Judaizers to impose the garbage of ceremonial observances upon the Gentile churches [cf *Gal* 5.12]. 'All "confidence in the flesh" is contemptuously cast aside and abhorred as dirty muck! [Cf *Is* 64.6; *Zech* 3.3–5] Such is God's estimate of all religious observance and practice which is not rooted in Christ and His atoning merit' (R. P. Martin, *TNTC*).

*V*8b: **that I may gain Christ, 9 and be found in him, not having a righteousness of mine own, *even* that which is of the law, but that which is through faith in Christ, the righteousness which is from God by faith:**

Paul's motive in reaching such a radical reassessment is to gain Christ and be found in him. Although many take this to be a reference to the final judgment (cf Moffatt: 'and be found at death in him'), the context clearly shows that Paul is thinking about his *present* interest in Christ and what is involved in thus finding himself 'incorporate in him' (NEB). Here he explains the meaning of union with Christ, first negatively, and then positively.

not having a righteousness of mine own, *even* that which is of the law, In this echo of the apostle's teaching in Romans and Galatians we have his mature judgment upon the years of fruitless striving to attain righteousness by his own fulfilment of the law's demands [cf *Rom* 3.19, 20; *Gal* 2.16, 21; 3.10]. His encounter with Christ had taught him that his legal righteousness was an external sham that would not pass muster with God, and the whole of his subsequent struggle against placing even a particle of faith in human merit was simply the outworking of that conversion-experience.

but that which is through faith in Christ, the righteousness which is from God by faith: 'But' marks a complete antithesis to such misplaced confidence in the flesh. The only way to attain a right standing with God is through the justifying faith that lays hold of Christ, whose obedience in life and death secured that perfect righteousness which is provided by God and received on the basis of faith [*Rom* 4.4–6, 23–25]. 'The contrast is between the righteousness which a man can make for himself and the righteousness that God gives him. And the contrast is absolute. . . . (Paul) founds salvation solely on an alien righteousness, with the express exclusion of every item of our own righteousness. . . . The Gospel, to Paul, consists precisely in this: that we do nothing to earn our salvation or to secure it for ourselves. God in Christ does it all' (B. B. Warfield, 'The Alien Righteousness' in *Faith and Life*, pp. 321–322).

V 10: **that I may know him, and the power of his resurrection, and the fellowship of his sufferings, becoming conformed unto his death; 11 if by any means I may attain unto the resurrection from the dead.**

that I may know him, (i.e. Christ) Having already spoken of the 'knowledge' of Christ [*v* 8], Paul now defines the content of the faith mentioned in the previous verse by explaining what is involved in knowing Christ [*v* 10b,c]. In sharp contrast to the perfectionists who claimed to have arrived at the goal [*vv* 12–16], Paul's great desire is to come to know Christ with ever increasing intimacy, even though that means choosing the way of suffering and death [1.29f].

and the power of his resurrection, This is placed first because it must come first in the order of Christian experience. The reference is not to the power by which

Christ was raised from the dead, but to the power which the resurrected Christ exerts over his people in raising them from the sepulchre of their sins to the newness of life in him [*Rom* 6.4ff; *Eph* 1.19ff; 2.5, 6; *Col* 3.1]. 'It is the power of the risen Christ as it becomes a subject of practical knowledge and a power in Paul's inner life' (Vincent, *ICC*, p. 104).

and the fellowship of his sufferings, becoming conformed unto his death; Union with Christ also means entering into the fellowship of his sufferings. Paul is not claiming a share in that redemptive travail which was Christ's alone, but is speaking of the afflictions he willingly endures for the sake of Christ and his gospel [cf *Col* 1.24]. 'In growing conformity with his death' (NEB) indicates that 'the process of conformity was advancing – like Him in suffering, like Him in death . . . in all things Paul coveted conformity to His Lord – even in suffering and death' (Eadie). [Cf *2 Cor* 7–11].

if by any means The phrase 'expresses not doubt, but rather the eagerness that strives by *all* ways to reach its end' (Gwynn).

I may attain unto the resurrection from the dead. Paul's use of this unique expression – 'the out-resurrection from the dead' – is doubtless dictated by a polemical purpose. It is a telling thrust against those who were claiming to be sinlessly perfect on the basis of their spiritual resurrection with Christ in baptism (so Martin). But complete conformity with Christ will not be attained until the day of his coming, when all believers, whether alive or asleep [*1 Cor* 15.52], will be glorified together [*v* 21]. Paul does not refer to the resurrection of the wicked, because in addressing believers he naturally speaks of their resurrection to glory [cf 1 *Cor* 15.20–23; 1 *Thess* 4.16, 17]. But that is no reason for supposing that the eternal destiny of the righteous and the wicked will be determined separately rather than at the same general resurrection [cf *Acts* 17.31f]. The resurrection is here represented as the goal of all Paul's striving, because it is only then that believers will be invested with the body of glory [*v* 21]. 'As no one can expect to stand in the last day who has not practised holiness in the fear of God, so no one can hope to attain unto the resurrection of life who has not learned to know Christ and the power of his resurrection and the fellowship of his sufferings, being conformed unto his death. Such a mode of viewing the resurrection need not do away with the other mode of viewing it as a gift of free grace bestowed for the sake of the merit of Christ' (G. Vos, *The Pauline Eschatology*, p. 257).

V 12: **Not that I have already obtained, or am already made perfect: but I press on, if so be that I may lay hold on that for which also I was laid hold on by Christ Jesus.**

In countering the false claims of the 'perfectionists', Paul appeals to his own experience to prove that believers are not made perfect in this present life, but he also insists that they must constantly strive for increasing conformity to Christ. The imagery used here is that of the foot-race. Paul runs the Christian race with all the dedication of an athlete who is bent on winning the prize. This gives us an interesting insight into the psychology of Christian perseverance. The man who is tempted to succumb to the snare of perfectionism will lapse into a state of spiritual complacency. He will consider that he has already arrived at the goal, and regard his fellow-believers as mere 'also rans' in the spiritual race! It is only the consciousness of not yet having arrived which will quicken our endeavours, just as the athlete strains every muscle to finish the course.

Not that I have already obtained, or am already made perfect: The first verb probably points to the time of Paul's conversion, while the second refers to his present state: 'Neither when I became Christ's did I attain, nor, up to this time, have I been perfected' (Vincent). Although 'obtained' has no object, the metaphor suggests that Paul has in view 'the prize' awarded to the victorious athlete [*v* 14].

but I press on, if so be that I may lay hold on that for which also I was laid hold on by Christ Jesus. It is in virtue of the grace received in his conversion that Paul still presses on to see if he can grasp the goal for which he was then grasped by Christ. As J. Dupont points out, Christ suddenly seized Paul in an *irresistible way*. 'If Paul is now on the race track, as he describes it in verses 13–14, he has to thank this "start" which came with the Damascus event' ('The Conversion of Paul' in *Apostolic History and the Gospel*, pp. 181, 191).

*V*13: **Brethren, I count not myself yet to have laid hold: but one thing** *I do,* **forgetting the things which are behind, and stretching forward to the things which are before,** 14 **I press on toward the goal unto the prize of the high calling of God in Christ Jesus.**

Brethren, I count not myself yet to have laid hold:

Paul uses the earnest address 'brethren' to introduce an important statement. His emphatic disclaimer is clearly intended to point a contrast with those who thought themselves 'perfect' [*v* 15]. The fact that the aged apostle does not even consider himself to be within reach of the prize should give the most convinced perfectionists in Philippi pause for thought, not to speak of their successors today!

but one thing *I do* **,** 'There is no need to supply a verb. His Christian conduct is summed up in what follows. Never has there been a more *unified* life than that of Paul as Apostle and Christian' (Kennedy).

forgetting the things which are behind, and stretching forward to the things which are before, As a *Pharisee* who thought he had arrived at perfection, Saul's present was determined by his past, for perfectionism is based on pride in one's progress in holiness [*vv* 4–6]. But as a *Christian*, Paul's present efforts are determined by his future goal, and so he forgets past achievements as he presses towards the prize. It is this forgetfulness of the past which frees us to run the Christian race. The competitor who is always looking back over his shoulder will never win that race. Many Christians are so paralysed by past failures or have become so complacent with past successes that they have virtually stopped running the race. But when with Paul we write off our past as a dead loss [*vv* 7, 8], then we are free to face the future with confidence. The formula for success in the Christian life is simple (but not *easy* like the 'instant' formula of the 'second blessing'!): relegate the past to oblivion, and *strain forward* for the prize which is set before us.

I press on toward the goal to win the prize for which God has called me heavenward in Christ Jesus. (NIV) Paul presses on because it is only when the goal is reached that the prize can be grasped. So he strives to attain the prize of 'perfect fellowship with Christ, and his glorification with Christ in the immaculate heritage of heaven hereafter [cf 2 *Tim* 4.8; *Rev* 2.10]. This prize is connected with the upward (heavenly, heavenward) call of God which he received at his conversion, when God's saving call to everlasting life came to him "in Christ Jesus", i.e. by His merit and in communion with Him' (J. J. Müller). The thought of this verse is well expressed in the familiar hymn, 'Fight the good fight':

> *Run the straight race through God's good grace,*
> *Lift up thine eyes, and seek His face;*
> *Life with its path before us lies;*
> *Christ is the way, and Christ the prize.*
>
> (J. S. B. Monsell)

V 15: **Let us therefore, as many as are perfect, be thus minded: and if in anything ye are otherwise minded, this also shall God reveal unto you:**

Let us therefore, as many as are perfect, be thus minded: Paul's gentle irony pinpoints the error of those who consider themselves to be 'perfect' as he picks up their favourite word, and in effect asks them to reconsider its meaning in the light of his personal testimony [*vv* 12–14]. He is quite prepared to include himself among the 'perfect' so long as they are 'thus minded', for only those who are conscious of their present imperfection will strive to attain the goal which still lies before them. The prospect of being 'perfect' is the Christian's hope; the claim 'to be already "perfect" is always recurring in various forms – all natural but unwarrantable anticipations of heaven on earth. St. Paul, by a striking paradox, bids those who hold themselves perfect to prove that they are so by a consciousness of imperfection. If they have it not, he says, they have something yet to learn' (Alfred Barry).

and if in anything ye are otherwise minded, this also shall God reveal unto you: Paul cannot regard the error of the perfectionists with indifference because he knows that to cherish such a delusion as the *truth* will result in misshapen conduct. As one who is sure that he possesses God's truth, the apostle assures those who doubtless boasted of their special 'revelations' that they still stand to profit from a further disclosure of divine truth, for God is sure to show them their mistake.

V 16: **only, whereunto we have attained, by that same *rule* let us walk.**

Only to what you have attained, with the same keep in line! (Lenski) In this exhortation to 'march in line', Paul seeks to safeguard the unity of the church by discouraging the idea that Christians are to be 'spiritual virtuosos' (F. W. Beare), each glorying in his own attainments without regard to the well-being of the body to which he belongs. 'He is anxious for two things – that they should keep on in one course, and that all should keep on together. In both senses he addresses the "perfect"; he will have them understand that they have attained only one thing – to be in the right path, and that it is for them to continue in it; he also bids them refrain from setting themselves up above "the imperfect"; for the very fact of division would mark them as still "carnal", mere "babes in Christ" [1 *Cor* 3.1–4]' (Barry).

V 17: **Brethren, be ye imitators together of me, and mark them that so walk even as ye have us for an ensample.**

By way of application [*vv* 7–14], Paul exhorts his brothers in the faith to be fellow-imitators of him. As an apostle, he is a man whose unique authority stems from his knowledge of Christ's will for the church, and so there is no egotism in thus presenting himself as an authentic pattern for believers to follow [cf 4.9]. But here he means something more than: 'Follow my example'. His primary emphasis is: 'Recognize my authority, follow what I say, be obedient' (so W. Michaelis, *TDNT*, Vol IV, p. 668).

and watch closely those who are walking according to the example that we have set you. (Hendriksen) In passing from the singular to the plural, Paul has in view the example set by his associates Timothy and Epaphroditus. For their leadership is also in accord with the standard laid down by himself, even though they do not share his special status as a divinely appointed apostle (Martin).

V 18: **For many walk, of whom I told you often, and now tell you even weeping, *that they are* the enemies of the cross of Christ: 19 whose end is perdition, whose god is the belly, and *whose* glory is in their shame, who mind earthly things.**

[83]

For many walk, of whom I told you often, The Philippians must imitate those who exemplify the faith they teach [*v* 17], for Paul had often warned them to be on their guard against an evil which was widespread among the Gentile churches, though it had not yet reached them [1.3–8]. The persons described are clearly 'professing Christians who allowed their liberty to degenerate into licence [*Gal* 5.13]; who, from an altogether superficial view of grace, thought lightly of continuing in sin [*Rom* 6.1, 12–13, 15, 23]; who, while bearing the name of Christ, were concerned only with their own self-indulgence [*Rom* 16.18]' (Kennedy).

and now tell you even weeping, The stress of Paul's 'grief would lie in the fact, that they degraded the true doctrine of liberty, so as to minister to their profligate and worldly living. They made use of his name, but did not follow his example' (Lightfoot).

that they are **the enemies of the cross of Christ:** Such libertines are indeed 'the enemies of the cross of Christ', for though they claim a saving interest in Christ crucified, their sinful lives are a flagrant denial of the faith they confess with their lips. 'The true Christian is the man who is "crucified with Christ", who has "crucified the flesh with its affections and lusts". The Cross is the central principle in his life. "If any man will come after me, let him deny himself and take up his cross and follow me". Those here described, by their unthinking self-indulgence, run directly in the teeth of this principle' (Kennedy).

whose end is perdition, Paul states the destiny of these men before specifying the nature of their conduct, so 'that what follows may be read with the greater horror' (Bengel). 'Perdition' points not to the extinction of existence, but to that state of utter ruin and everlasting torment, which is the only appropriate 'end' for the ungodly [2 *Thess* 1.9; 2 *Pet* 3.7, 16].

whose god is the belly, Perhaps under the influence of an incipient gnosticism, these 'men of the Spirit' felt that they could indulge their bodily appetites without restraint [1 *Cor* 6.13], and so surrendered themselves to gluttony and licentiousness.

and *whose* glory is in their shame, Although they 'gloried' in their freedom to do as they pleased, they did not realize that such slavery to their lusts meant that they were glorying in their 'shame'.

who mind earthly things. Finally, Paul expresses his amazement at professed believers whose mental horizon was bounded by earthly things! 'In a parallel passage the apostle shows us what these *earthly things* were on which these people set their minds, namely, immorality, indecency, lust, evil desire, greed, evil temper, furious rage, malice, cursing, filthy talk [*Col* 3.2, 5, 8]' (Hendriksen).

*V*20: **For our citizenship is in heaven; whence also we wait for a Saviour, the Lord Jesus Christ:**

This advances the reason for rejecting such a misinterpretation of Christian liberty: 'for *our* commonwealth is in heaven' (ASV margin). Since the Philippians lived in a colony whose citizens regarded distant Rome as their native city, they would be quick to grasp Paul's metaphor which shows that heaven is the true homeland of believers (see comment on 1.27). As aliens who have here no continuing city, their life is not rooted in 'earthly things' to which they owe no allegiance, for they belong by the adoption of grace to that heavenly city 'whose architect and builder is God' [Heb 11.10, NIV; cf Gal 4.26; Eph 2.19; 1 Pet 2.11]. It is because the Christian's affections are centred upon 'the things that are above' that his earthly walk will be very different from the walk of those whose minds are still captivated by what is purely temporal [Col 3.1-3].

whence also we wait for a Saviour, the Lord Jesus Christ: Moreover, it is from heaven that we eagerly await the advent of a *Saviour*, for it is in his capacity as Saviour that the Lord Jesus Christ will complete our final deliverance [v 21]. Instead of pinning their hopes upon the doubtful divinity of an earthly emperor, believers look for the coming of a Saviour, who has the power both to free them from the bondage of death, and to bestow upon them the glorious liberty of the children of God [Rom 8.21].

*V*21: **who shall fashion anew the body of our humiliation, *that it may be* conformed to the body of his glory, according to the working whereby he is able even to subject all things unto himself.**

In contrast to the false claims of the perfectionists, Paul here shows that the tension between the 'already' and the 'not yet' of the Christian's present state can only be resolved when Christ returns to glorify his people. But the fact that the 'prize' of perfection must be bestowed by an act of divine power offers no loophole for the spiritually lazy, for in the meantime all believers must be like the Olympic

[86]

athlete who spares no effort to attain the goal which still lies before him [*vv* 11–14].

who shall fashion anew the body of our humiliation, *that it may be* conformed to the body of his glory, Far from entertaining the Greek notion of the body as being the tomb of the soul, Paul cannot conceive of any salvation which does not embrace the *whole* man, yet his doctrine of the resurrection is no abstract theory but the living truth of his own experience. In his encounter with the Risen Christ he witnessed the óbjective reality of 'the body of his glory', while his subjective insight into the significance of this truth was imparted to him by the inward illumination of the Spirit [*Gal* 1.16]. By way of contrast, he calls our present body 'the body of our humiliation' because it is subject to frailty, sinfulness, mortality, and corruption. As in 2.6–8, the compounds used here mark the difference between what is external and transitory ('fashion') and what is essential and permanent ('form'). Paul thus 'declares a future change of *outward fashion* of body, to result in a full *assimilation of form* (implying the whole *nature*) of the risen Christian to his glorified Lord. He has told us [*v* 10] of the gradual process by which the Christian is, in this life, *in course of conforming* to Christ's death. That process, we here learn, is to be consummated by the *change of fashion* of the body, from the natural to the spiritual [1 *Cor* 15.44], in the Resurrection. Then the entire man, body and soul, shall be *conformable*, – assimilated alike in outward aspect and in inward verity, to the Glory of the Lord' (Gwynn).

according to the working whereby he is able even to subject all things unto himself. The miracle of the resurrection will be accomplished by the same omnipotent power which enables Christ to bring all things under his rule [2.10, 11]. 'His is a sovereign power to which all things are subordinate – all earthly power and authority, enemies and death [cf 1 *Cor* 15.24–27; *Eph* 1.21, 22]' (Müller).

CHAPTER FOUR

In calling for steadfastness and unity, Paul begs Euodia and Syntyche to resolve their differences, and bids them all to rejoice in the Lord as they show that forbearance towards others which befits those who know that the Lord is at hand [vv 1–5]. They are to be anxious about nothing, for if they commit their needs to God in prayer, the peace of God will guard their hearts and thoughts in Christ Jesus [vv 6, 7]. Finally, he exhorts them to practise every kind of moral goodness, and again urges them to follow his example [vv 8, 9]. Paul thanks them for their ministry to him in prison, although he has learned to be content in all circumstances through the Lord's enabling power [vv 10–13]. Their fellowship in his affliction reminds him of their earlier generosity, and he describes the gift they sent with Epaphroditus as an acceptable sacrifice to God [vv 14–20]. Believers in Caesar's household are specially mentioned in the final greeting, and the letter closes with the usual benediction [vv 21–23].

*V*1: **Wherefore, my brethren beloved and longed for, my joy and crown, so stand fast in the Lord, my beloved.**

It is unfortunate that this chapter begins with an exhortation which should be regarded as the proper conclusion of the preceding appeal [3.17ff]. Paul's close attachment to the church at Philippi is shown by his multiplied expressions of love. He not only addresses them as 'my brethren beloved and longed for', but in calling them 'my joy and crown' he lets them know that his joy is bound up with their steadfast perseverance in the faith. 'The Philippian converts are his chaplet of victory, showing that he has not run in vain, ch 2.16' (Vincent). Paul bases his admonition upon the fact of their union with Christ, so that the call to 'stand fast in the Lord' also reveals the secret of such stability [cf *Eph* 6.10]. 'So stand' means live in accordance with the pattern just set forth [3.17–21], 'as you are guided by my precept and my example, as becomes citizens of a heavenly kingdom' (Lightfoot).

*V*2: **I exhort Euodia, and I exhort Syntyche, to be of the same mind in the Lord.**

Having carefully prepared the ground by stressing the need for unity and humility throughout the letter [1.27; 2.1–5, 14], Paul is at last ready to deal with a sharp personality clash between two prominent women whose quarrel evidently threatened the peace and harmony of the whole church [*v* 3]. It is sad to think that our introduction to Euodia and Syntyche is due to the fact that they were at odds with one another. This is the kind of dubious notoriety we would do well to shun! Paul scrupulously avoids taking sides in the dispute and calls upon both women 'to be of the same mind in the Lord', thus making a pointed personal application of his previous admonition to the church [2.2]. To share the Lord's mind involves the adoption of the same attitude of self-sacrificing love [2.5]. As pride is the root cause of such divisions within the church, so humility is the sole remedy for this all too frequent distemper. For the disease can be arrested only when Christians are humble enough to renounce self-interest and take a genuine interest in the concerns of others [2.3, 4]. 'In the Lord' characterizes 'the specifically *Christian* concord, the moral nature and effort of which are grounded on Christ as their determining vital principle. Paul does not desire a union of minds *apart from* Christ' (Meyer).

V 3: **Yea, I beseech thee also, true yokefellow, help these women, for they laboured with me in the gospel, with Clement also, and the rest of my fellow-workers, whose names are in the book of life.**

It is impossible to identify the person whom Paul calls his 'true yokefellow', and the suggestion that this designation be regarded as a proper name (Syzygus, who is asked to live up to his name in uniting these women) is improbable since the word is nowhere else used as a proper name. However, the Philippians would know whom Paul meant, and this partner is urged to help Euodia and Syntyche in resolving their differences, for they shared in Paul's struggles to establish the church at Philippi [*Acts* 16.13], together with Clement (who is otherwise unknown to us) and the rest of the fellow-workers, 'whose names are in the book of life'. This is intended as an excuse 'for not inserting them here; their names (says he) are written in a much more excellent book than this Epistle of mine. This "Book of Life", of which he speaks, is the register of the kingdom of heaven, wherein are enrolled the names of all the elect. . . . For the Scripture, employing frequently things of earth in order to represent to our minds the things of heaven, compares the list of the people of God, whom He has chosen from eternity, and marked as His elect, to a register, in which the names of all the citizens of a town are enrolled. I confess that to us this book is shut up and sealed. God knows them that are His, but will not manifest them fully until that day when the books shall be opened and the sheep separated from the goats. But meanwhile we may judge, although with modesty and charity, by the actions of men, and hold as the elect of God, as citizens of the new Jerusalem, truly enrolled in its registers, those who display in their lives the marks of Divine adoption, such as faith, obedience, love, holiness, perseverance, and other graces. And therefore the apostle scruples not to say, that the "names" of the Philippians in whose conduct and conversation he had observed these holy qualities were written in the "Book of Life" (Daillé).

*V*4: **Rejoice in the Lord always: again I will say, Rejoice.**

Paul here returns to the dominant note of the Epistle as he reissues the call to rejoice in the Lord which he repeats for emphasis [3.1]. 'He doubles it to take away the scruple of those that might say, What, shall we rejoice in afflictions?' (G. Herbert cited by Kennedy). They are to rejoice *always*, for 'in the Lord' there is abundant cause for rejoicing even from the depths of a Roman dungeon [cf *Acts* 16.25; *Rom* 8.28, 35ff]. 'No duty almost more pressed in both Testaments than this of rejoicing in the Lord. It is no less a sin not to rejoice than not to repent' (Trapp).

*V*5: **Let your forbearance be known unto all men. The Lord is at hand.**

The Philippians must not be so preoccupied with their

own internal problems as to lose sight of their impact upon the world. Hence Paul urges them to become known for their 'forbearance' to all men. In their relations with others they are to show a gracious and gentle spirit which does not insist upon its rights, since they know that the Lord's coming will vindicate their cause. Because they are assured of heavenly glory, they can afford to be forbearing 'towards all men in spite of every persecution. Faith in their hidden, heavenly plenitude of light and power and life produces a saving gentleness. It is the earthly counterpart of the heavenly glory. Hence it is not weakness or sentimentality. It is the earthly outworking of an eschatological possession [cf *Phil* 2.15–16]' (H. Preisker, *TDNT*, Vol II, p. 590). Thus the expectation of the parousia should promote an ethical response of the kind which is a far cry from the unhealthy excitement it so often fosters in those who are more interested in date-fixing than in walking 'worthily of the Lord unto all pleasing' [*Col* 1.10].

*V*6: **In nothing be anxious; but in everything by prayer and supplication with thanksgiving let your requests be made known unto God.**

Paul's familiarity with the teaching of his Lord is shown in this warning against being distracted by anxiety [*Matt* 6.25–34]. Instead of giving way to such carking care, the Philippians are to commit everything to God in prayer. As they lay their specific requests before God, they are to make their supplication with thanksgiving for past mercies and present blessings [*Col* 4.2]. 'Because many often pray to God amiss, with complaints or murmurings, as though they had just ground for accusing Him, while others cannot brook delay if He does not immediately obey their wishes,

Paul joins thanksgiving with prayers. It is as though he had said that those things which are necessary for us ought to be desired from the Lord in such a way that we nevertheless subject our affections to His will, and give thanks while asking. And, unquestionably, gratitude will have the effect upon us that the will of God will be the chief sum of our desires' (Calvin).

*V*7: **And the peace of God, which passeth all understanding, shall guard your hearts and your thoughts in Christ Jesus.**

And This has consecutive force: 'and so'. It introduces the blessed result, 'which the compliance with verse 6 will have for the inner man' (Meyer).

the peace of God, This inward peace is bestowed on the basis of Christ's objective achievement, for peace *from* God is founded upon the work of reconciliation which established peace *with* God [*Rom* 5.1; *Eph* 2.14ff]. 'We cannot think of the one, indeed, without thinking of the other; nor can one exist apart from the other. We cannot have peace of heart, until our real and actual separation from God is bridged by the blood of Christ. We cannot have the breach between God and us healed without a sense of the new relation of peace stealing into our hearts' (B. B. Warfield, 'Peace with God' in *Faith and Life*, p. 329).

which surpasses every (human) **reason,** (Vincent) In its power to relieve anxiety the peace of God surpasses all our futile attempts to 'reason' our cares away. 'God's peace produces far better results than human scheming; it is superior to all man's devices for security, and is more efficacious in removing disquietude than any intellectual effort or reasoning power. These often augment disquietude' (Plummer).

shall guard your hearts and your thoughts The city of Philippi was guarded by a Roman garrison, so Paul's metaphor would appeal to his readers. 'The peace of God is the garrison of the soul in all the experiences of its life, defending it from the external assaults of temptation or anxiety, and disciplining all lawless desires and imaginations within, that war against its higher purposes' (Kennedy).

in Christ Jesus. God's peace is realized only in union with Christ Jesus, and this relationship requires believers to submit to his gracious rule over their lives [cf *Col* 3.15].

*V*8: **Finally, brethren, whatsoever things are true, whatsoever things are honourable, whatsoever things are just, whatsoever things are pure, whatsoever things are lovely, whatsoever things are of good report; if there be any virtue, and if there be any praise, think on these things.**

In bringing the letter to a close, Paul urges his brothers in the faith to cultivate those good qualities which will command the admiration of their heathen neighbours, though *they* know nothing of the grace that enables believers to manifest such virtues.

whatsoever things are true, Whatever is 'true' must be understood in the widest sense of all that is true in thought, word, and deed. 'They are to think on "the true" in everything of which it can be predicated – both in reference to God and man, the church and the world, themselves and others – the true in its spiritual and secular relations, in thought, speech, and position' (Eadie).

whatsoever things are honourable, The word used here comes from the verb 'to worship', and so means 'reverend' (ASV margin), or 'venerable' in the sense of 'worthy of honour'. 'As the Christian is a child of God, an heir of heaven, a brother of the Lord Jesus, a fellow-citizen with the angels, the salt of the earth, and the light of the world, the master and teacher of all men, it is clear that such high qualities must oblige him to maintain a holy and grave deportment; and that he could not fall in with the opposite vices, without betraying his honour and scandalously belying his profession' (Daillé).

whatsoever things are just, 'Just' should not be restricted to just dealing with men, but must be taken in its broadest meaning: 'whatsoever things are in accordance with eternal and unchanging rectitude' (Eadie).

whatsoever things are pure, Not merely chaste, but pure in the most comprehensive sense. Whatever things are pure: 'which are neither tainted nor corrupt – free from all debasing elements, clear in nature, transparent in purpose, leaving no blot on the conscience and no stain on the character' (Eadie).

whatsoever things are lovely, 'Lovely', which is found only here in the New Testament, refers to whatever others find worthy of admiration and love. 'The apostle speaks only of such things as are not contrary to the will of God, while at the same time they are agreeable and pleasing to men. In this class I would place patience, cheerfulness, sweetness of temper, generosity, and such-like virtues. For although all virtues are beautiful and excellent in themselves, and deserve the approbation and respect of men, being all emanations from God and the fruits of His Spirit, yet nevertheless there are some more pleasing than others' (Daillé).

whatsoever things are of good report; The alternatives offered in Arndt-Gingrich highlight the difficulty of translating this word which also occurs only here in the New Testament. According to Vincent, the meaning is not 'well spoken of', but 'fair-speaking', and so 'winning' or 'gracious'. Thus 'whatever is of gracious import' would involve 'expressing what is kind and likely to win people, and avoiding what is likely to give offence' (Plummer).

if there be any virtue, and if there be any praise, think on these things. By switching to conditional clauses, Paul directs the Philippians to exercise their own discernment in approving the things which are morally excellent and worthy of public acclaim. But to 'think on these things' means more than simply meditating upon them [v 9]. 'He desires us to "think" of them, because the mind is the root of all human actions. It is the mind which influences the will, stirs up the affections, and conceives and produces every action. He therefore would have the act follow the intention. For it is not merely to indulge the mind in the pleasure of vain speculations that we are to exercise ourselves in this lofty study, but rather that we may put in practice all that we have understood' (Daillé).

*V*9: **The things which ye both learned and received and heard and saw in me, these things do: and the God of peace shall be with you.**

Paul here presents his own teaching and example as a pattern for the Philippians to follow. 'Learned and received' refer to their instruction in the gospel 'traditions' which he had handed down to them with all the authority of an apostle [cf 1 *Cor* 11.2, 15.1ff; *Gal* 1.9; 1 *Thess* 4.1, 2; 2 *Thess* 2.15]. 'Heard and saw' refer to their experience of his personal conduct both in word and deed. If they do these things, then 'the God of peace' will be with them. 'Not only the peace of God, *v* 7, but God himself' (Bengel).

*V*10: **But I rejoice in the Lord greatly, that now at length ye have revived your thought for me; wherein ye did indeed take thought, but ye lacked opportunity.**

With rare tact and delicacy, Paul expresses his deep appreciation of the gift the Philippians had sent with Epaphroditus, while at the same time maintaining the independence he had found through depending upon Christ for all things [*vv* 10–18]. 'The passage presents as tactful a treatment of a delicate matter as can well be found in the whole range of high literature' (H. von Soden).

Now I rejoice in the Lord greatly that now at length you caused your concern for my welfare to bloom afresh; (Hendriksen) In expressing his great joy in the Lord at the Philippians' revived concern for his welfare, Paul uses a verb which suggests the image of a tree putting forth fresh shoots in the Spring. As this might seem like a reproach for a 'winter of neglect', he at once proceeds to absolve them from any blame by acknowledging that, though their concern for him was constant, they had lacked the opportunity to give it practical expression. Perhaps this was due to their uncertainty regarding the apostle's movements in recent years, or it may have been because they had no one to send with their gift.

*V*11: **Not that I speak in respect of want: for I have learned, in whatsoever state I am, therein to be content.**

Although Paul is touched by his friends' practical concern for his welfare, he hastens to dispel any thought of dependence upon their generosity, for he has learned the secret of being content whatever the circumstances. The word 'content' literally means 'self-sufficient', and the Stoics used it of the man who had cultivated an inward detachment from all things and all people, which enabled him to face whatever life brought to him with unshaken resolve. But whereas the Stoic boasted of his self-sufficiency, Paul finds his sufficiency in Christ whose power gives him the victory even in the midst of adversity [*v* 13]. 'The contentment which the apostle universally and uniformly possessed, sprang not from indifference, apathy, or desperation . . . It was no egotistic delusion that upheld him, nor did he ever invoke the storm to show that he could brave it. But his mind calmly bowed to the will of God in every condition in which he was placed. For that wondrous equanimity and cheerfulness which far excelled the stolid and stubborn endurance ascribed to heathen stoicism, gave him the mastery over circumstances. He felt the evil, but surmounted it – a purer triumph than with a petrified heart to be unconscious of it' (Eadie).

*V*12: **I know how to be abased, and I know also how to abound: in everything and in all things have I learned the secret both to be filled and to be hungry, both to abound and to be in want.**

Paul knows from personal experience both how to endure privations and to enjoy an abundance. Since his resources are in Christ, he is neither overwhelmed by poverty nor intoxicated by prosperity. In every situation of life, his serenity is undisturbed because he has learned the secret of true contentment. 'Plenty and hunger, abundance and want – in all these Paul has been initiated. He knows the joys and the cares of life, prosperity and adversity, "good" days and "evil" days, favourable and unfavourable circumstances. And he has learned to be content under all circumstances, be they good or be they evil' (Müller).

*V*13: **I can do all things in him that strengtheneth me.**

What apparently begins as Paul's comprehensive claim to self-sufficiency ('I can do all things'), paradoxically concludes as an expression of his entire dependence upon Christ ('in him who infuses strength into me'). This great affirmation of faith has been of inestimable comfort to countless Christians down the ages. 'The self-sufficiency of the Christian is relative: an independence of the world through dependence upon God. The Stoic self-sufficiency pretends to be absolute. One is the contentment of faith, the other of pride' (G. G. Findlay).

*V*14: **Howbeit ye did well that ye had fellowship with my affliction.**

Paul here resumes his thankful recognition of the gift the Philippians had sent to him. For in declaring his independence of human aid, he did not wish to disparage their generosity which gladdened his heart, because he regarded their sacrifice as a noble deed in which they had made common cause with his affliction. By their active support of the imprisoned apostle, they became sharers in the struggle to fulfil his vocation. 'They helped him to carry his burden by means of their material gift, their fellow-feeling and intercession, their interest and their willingness to make sacrifices, and so they had a share in alleviating his hardship in captivity' (Müller). [cf 1.5]

V 15: **And ye yourselves also know, ye Philippians, that in the beginning of the gospel, when I departed from Macedonia, no church had fellowship with me in the matter of giving and receiving but ye only; 16 for even in Thessalonica ye sent once and again unto my need.**

With an upsurge of affection for his beloved friends ('ye Philippians'), Paul gratefully acknowledges that the gift brought by Epaphroditus was not the first he had received from them. For he recalls that not long after their coming to faith in Christ ('in the beginning of the gospel'), when he departed from Macedonia to evangelize Achaia, no other church had shared with him in the cost of that mission [2 *Cor* 11.9]. 'In the matter of giving and receiving' they alone had provided practical support in *giving* what Paul had been glad to *receive*. And even while he was still in Macedonia, they had sent gifts to supply his need on more than one occasion during his stay at Thessalonica.

V 17: **Not that I seek for the gift; but I seek for the fruit that increaseth to your account.**

In thus enlarging upon past generosity Paul wishes to make clear that he is not seeking further gifts [*v* 18]. 'It is not the gift he covets, but that rich spiritual blessing which the gift secures to its donor' (Eadie). For he sees their gift as a kind of investment in which 'the fruit' or 'interest' is accumulating to their credit. It was Paul's constant aim to enrich his converts by encouraging their growth in grace, and as the Philippians' gift was a tangible evidence of that grace, he is confident that their sacrificial service will be amply rewarded at the last day [cf 1.11].

V 18: **But I have all things, and abound: I am filled, having received from Epaphroditus the things** *that came* **from you, an odour of a sweet smell, a sacrifice acceptable, well-pleasing to God.**

However, here I give you my receipt for everything – for more than everything; I am paid in full, now that I have received from Epaphroditus what you sent. (NEB) Paul here continues his playful use of commercial metaphors to show that the Philippians have fully discharged their 'debt' to him [2.25–30]. A. Deissmann has shown that the verb 'I have' (meaning 'I have received') frequently occurs in the papyri as a technical expression for the drawing up of a receipt.

an odour of a sweet smell, a sacrifice acceptable, well-pleasing to God. But though Paul is grateful for their gift, his sudden switch to the vocabulary of sacrifice reminds them that its greatest value lay in what it meant to God. It is a fragrant offering that is pleasing to God [*Gen* 8.21; *Lev* 1.9]. What was given to meet Paul's needs was in fact an acceptable act of worship [*Rom* 12.1], and Collange points out that this says something about church 'offerings' which deserves consideration.

V 19: **And my God shall supply every need of yours according to his riches in glory in Christ Jesus.**

And my God will meet all your needs according to his glorious riches in Christ Jesus. (NIV) As the Philippians have made an offering to God in meeting the needs of his servant, so *his* God will abundantly recompense them by meeting all their needs 'according to', i.e. on a scale that befits his glorious riches in Christ Jesus. God is no man's debtor, and he will not fail to supply the needs of those who gladly make sacrifices to forward his cause in the world.

V 20: **Now unto our God and Father *be* the glory for ever and ever. Amen.**

As worship is the only fitting response to God's bounty, Paul concludes this section of his letter with a doxology, in which he invites his readers to join him in ascribing glory 'to our God and Father' who so wonderfully provides for the needs of his children. This tribute of praise shall endure 'unto the ages of the ages' (ASV margin) – 'an image taken from the cycles or calendars of time, to represent an immeasurable eternity' (Eadie). The truth thus expressed is endorsed by the confessional 'Amen'.

*V*21: **Salute every saint in Christ Jesus. The brethren that are with me salute you.**

Paul probably wrote the final words of the Epistle in his own hand [2 *Thess* 3.17]. His closing greeting is unique in that he mentions no one by name, yet he includes everyone by using the singular 'every saint' instead of the usual plural. No doubt this is because he wishes to avoid the appearance of favouring particular individuals when writing to a church which has been suffering from personality clashes between some of its members [4.2]. But there should be no disunity in the church where every saint is 'in Christ Jesus', and Paul's greeting is intended to cement that unity. As the verb 'greet' lacks a subject, it is difficult to decide how this greeting was to be conveyed. Perhaps through the leaders of the church as Vincent suggests, but more probably Paul intends the Philippians to greet one another (so Martin). The brethren with Paul, who also send their greetings, are presumably 'the companions who visited him most frequently in his imprisonment, especially Timothy' (Plummer).

*V*22: **All the saints salute you, especially they that are of Caesar's household.**

All the Christians in Rome also send their greetings, especially those who belong to Caesar's household, i.e. those engaged in the service of Nero, whether as slaves or freedmen. 'This is worthy of notice; for it is no common evidence of divine mercy that the Gospel had penetrated that sink of all crimes and iniquities. It is also the more wonderful, because it is a rare thing for holiness to reign in courts' (Calvin).

*V*23: **The grace of the Lord Jesus Christ be with your spirit.**

In the concluding benediction Paul prays for the grace of the Lord Jesus Christ to be with 'your' (plural) 'spirit' (singular). This provides another hint that his paramount concern is to have the whole church united in one spirit. They are all to work together as one person. 'In their whole inner being, in all their thoughts and desires, they must continually share and experience the grace of the Lord' (Greijdanus cited by Müller).

Soli Deo Gloria

BIBLIOGRAPHY

Arndt, W. F., and Gingrich, F. W., *A Greek-English Lexicon of the New Testament* (University of Chicago Press, 1957)

Barry, Alfred, *The Epistles to the Ephesians, Philippians, and Colossians* (A Bible Commentary for English Readers, Edited by C. J. Ellicott, Vol. VIII) (Cassell, nd)

Beare, F. W., *The Epistle to the Philippians* (A & C Black, 1973)

Bengel, J. A., *New Testament Word Studies* (Kregel, 1971)

Berkhof, L., *The History of Christian Doctrines* (Banner of Truth, 1969)

Bruce, F. F., *Paul: Apostle of the Free Spirit* (Paternoster Press, 1977)

Bruce, F. F., *An Expanded Paraphrase of the Epistles of Paul* (Paternoster Press, 1965)

Caird, G. B., *Paul's Letters from Prison* (OUP, 1976)

Calvin, John, *Galatians – Colossians* (St. Andrew Press, 1965) (Translator, T. H. L. Parker)

Collange, Jean-François, *The Epistle of Saint Paul to the Philippians* (Translated by A. W. Heathcote) (Epworth Press)

Daillé, Jean, *An Exposition of Philippians* (Tyndale Bible Society, nd)

Douglas, J. D. (Editor), *The New Bible Dictionary* (IVP, 1962)

Eadie, John, *A Commentary on the Greek Text of the Epistle of Paul to the Philippians* (James and Klock, 1977)

Fergusson, James, *The Epistles of Paul* (Banner of Truth, 1978)

Gasque, W. Ward, and Martin, Ralph P. (Editors), *Apostolic History and the Gospel* (Paternoster Press, 1970)

[106]

Guthrie, Donald, *New Testament Introduction* (Tyndale, 1970)

Gwynn, J., *The Epistle to the Philippians* (Speaker's Commentary) (John Murray, 1881)

Jeremias, Joachim, *Jerusalem in the Time of Jesus* (SCM, 1969)

Jones, Maurice, *The Epistle to the Philippians* (WC) (Methuen, 1918)

Hagner, D. A., and Harris, M. J. (Editors), *Pauline Studies: Essays Presented to F. F. Bruce* (Paternoster Press, 1980)

Hendriksen, William, *The Epistle to the Philippians* (Banner of Truth, 1963)

Hunter, Archibald M., *Galatians – Colossians* (LBC) (John Knox Press, 1959)

Hunter, Archibald M., *Paul and His Predecessors* (Nicholson and Watson, 1940)

Kennedy, H. A. A., *The Epistle to the Philippians* (EGT) (Eerdmans, 1974)

Kent, Homer A., *Philippians* (EBC) (Zondervan, 1978)

Kittel, G. and Friedrich, G., *Theological Dictionary of the New Testament* Vols. I–X (Eerdmans, 1964–76) (Translated by Geoffrey W. Bromiley; Index by Ronald E. Pitkin)

Kümmel, W. G., *Introduction to the New Testament* (Revised Edition) (SCM, 1975)

Ladd, George Eldon, *A Theology of the New Testament* (Eerdmans, 1974)

Lane, W. L., *Ephesians – 2 Thessalonians* (Scripture Union, 1974)

Lenski, R. C. H., *The Interpretation of St. Paul's Epistles to the Galatians, to the Ephesians and to the Philippians* (Augsburg, 1961)

Lightfoot, J. B., *St. Paul's Epistle to the Philippians* (Zondervan, 1953)

Loh, I-Jin, and Nida, Eugene A., *A Translators' Handbook on Paul's Letter to the Philippians* (UBS, 1977)

Longenecker, Richard N., *The Christology of Early Jewish Christianity* (Baker, 1981)

MacLeod, Donald, *Philippians 2 and Christology* (TSF, nd)

Marshall, I. Howard, *The Origins of New Testament Christology* (IVP, 1976)

BIBLIOGRAPHY

Marshall, I. Howard, 'The Christ-Hymn in Philippians 2.5–11', *Tyndale Bulletin*, 1968, No. 19, pp. 104–127

Marshall, L. H., *The Challenge of New Testament Ethics* (Macmillan, 1946)

Martin, Ralph P., *The Epistle of Paul to the Philippians* (Tyndale, 1959)

Martin, Ralph P., *An Early Christian Confession* (Tyndale, 1960)

Martin, Ralph P., *Carmen Christi: Philippians 2.5–11 in Recent Interpretation and in the Setting of Early Christian Worship* (CUP, 1967)

Martin, Ralph P., *Philippians* (NCB) (Eerdmans, 1980)

Meyer, H. A. W., *The Epistles to the Philippians and Colossians* (Meyer NTC) (T & T Clark, 1879)

Michael, J. Hugh, *The Epistle to the Philippians* (MNTC) (Hodder & Stoughton, 1943)

Müller, J. J., *The Epistles of Paul to the Philippians and to Philemon* (NICNT) (Eerdmans, 1955)

Murray, John, *The Collected Writings* Vol. III (Banner of Truth, 1982)

Neill, Stephen, *Christian Holiness* (Lutterworth, 1960)

Plummer, Alfred, *A Commentary on St. Paul's Epistle to the Philippians* (Fleming H. Revell, nd)

Ramsay, W. M., *St. Paul the Traveller and the Roman Citizen* (Hodder & Stoughton, 1900)

Robertson, A. T., *Word Pictures in the New Testament* Vol. IV (Broadman Press, 1931)

Scott, Ernest F., *The Epistle to the Philippians* (IB) (Abingdon, 1955)

Sherwin-White, A. N., *Roman Society and Roman Law in the New Testament* (Baker, 1978)

Stagg, Frank, *Philippians* (BBC) (Broadman Press, 1971)

Stanton, G. N., *Jesus of Nazareth in New Testament Preaching* (CUP, 1974)

Stauffer, Ethelbert, *New Testament Theology* (SCM, 1955)

Synge, F. C., *Philippians and Colossians* (Torch) (SCM, 1958)

Taylor, Vincent, *The Person of Christ in New Testament Teaching* (Macmillan, 1963)

Trapp, John, *Commentary on the New Testament* (Sovereign Grace Book Club, 1958)

Trench, R. C., *Synonyms of the New Testament* (James Clarke, 1961)

Vincent, Marvin R., *The Epistles to the Philippians and to Philemon* (ICC) (T & T Clark, 1972)

Vincent, Marvin R., *Word Studies in the New Testament* (MacDonald, nd)

Vos, Geerhardus, *The Pauline Eschatology* (Baker, 1979)

Warfield, B. B., *The Person and Work of Christ* (Presbyterian & Reformed, 1950)

Warfield, B. B., *Perfectionism* (Presbyterian & Reformed, 1958)

Warfield, B. B., *The Saviour of the World* (Mack Publishing, 1972)

Warfield, B. B., *The Lord of Glory* (Evangelical Press, 1974)

Warfield, B. B., *Faith and Life* (Banner of Truth, 1974)